Where Art Thou?

Where Art Thou?

Kenneth L. Neal

Northwest Publishing Inc.
Salt Lake City, Utah

Where Art Thou?

All rights reserved.
Copyright © 1992 Northwest Publishing, Inc.

Reproductions in any manner, in whole or in part,
in English or in other languages, or otherwise
without written permission of the publisher is prohibited.

This is a work of fiction.
All characters and events portrayed in this book are fictional,
and any resemblance to real people or incidents is purely coincidental.
For information address: Northwest Publishing, Inc.
6906 South 300 West, Salt Lake City, Utah 84047

MD 1992

PRINTING HISTORY
Second Printing 1994

ISBN: 1-880416-50-6

NPI books are published by Northwest Publishing, Incorporated,
6906 South 300 West, Salt Lake City, Utah 84047.
The name "NPI" and the "NPI" logo are trademarks belonging to
Northwest Publishing, Incorporated.

PRINTED IN THE UNITED STATES OF AMERICA.
10 9 8 7 6 5 4 3 2 1

Table of Contents

Acknowledgments		i
Foreword		ii
Introduction		iii
Definitions		ix
Chapter 1	"O God, Where Art Thou?"	1
Chapter 2	"Peace Be Unto Thy Soul"	9
Chapter 3	"Endure It Well"	19
Chapter 4	"Thou Art Not Yet As Job"	35
Chapter 5	"A Time Appointed For Every Man"	45
Chapter 6	"God Shall Give You Knowledge"	53
Chapter 7	"Nothing Shall Be Withheld"	61
Chapter 8	"Who Have Endured Valiantly"	73
Chapter 9	"Few Are Chosen"	87
Chapter 10	"They Do Not Learn This One Lesson"	99
Chapter 11	"Rights Of The Priesthood"	111
Chapter 12	"The Spirit Of The Lord Is Grieved"	127
Chapter 13	"Christ-like Attributes	141
Chapter 14	"The Doctrine Of The Priesthood"	187

Chapter 15   "The Holy Ghost Shall Be Thine?"   .   .   . 203
Chapter 16   "What Power Shall Stay The Heavens?"   .   . 223

Foreword

One of my most favorite experiences was discovered when I was reading the journal of Heber C. Kimball. He, along with John Taylor and Brigham Young, was an absolute stalwart in supporting, sustaining, and serving the Lord and His Prophet of the Dispensation of the Fulness of Times - Joseph Smith, Junior.

The Prophet gathered together a wagon train to go to the relief of the desperate Saints in Zion's Camp. Despite numerous spiritual experiences, many of the members wavered in their faith and testimony during that thousand-mile journey.

Those stalwarts mentioned above, and a few others like unto them, sharpened their faith in the Lord and their willingness to serve the Prophet. They "refined" their testimonies and their commitment to the Savior's great work during that long trek. But was that enough? No! They had to be tested some more.

Upon arriving at Zion's Camp, Heber C. Kimball was caught up in the illnesses that were rampant there - cholera and dysentery. He himself was stricken with cholera. In his own words, he wrote in his dairy: "I was seized by the hand of the destroyer, as I went in the woods to pray. I was instantly struck blind, and saw no way whereby I could free myself from the disease, only by jumping and thrashing myself about, until my sight returned to me and my blood began to circulate in my veins. I started and ran some distance, and by this means, through the help of God, I was enabled to extricate myself from the grasp of death."

Heber C. Kimball's trial of faith was complete. His offering, like Abraham's, had been accepted. He, and others, had been weighed in the eternal balance, and were not found wanting. Are we greater than they?

Each of us can expect to have an experience like unto Abraham or Heber C. Kimball. It will most likely occur in our lives **after** we have fully consecrated ourselves completely to God. In order to endure this, we must not reserve our free agency by partially surrendering ourselves to our covenants. When we make our commitments with no reservations, we will be tested. *"For all those who will not endure chastening, but deny me, cannot be sanctified"* (see D&C 101:5).

Since being called to work in the Salt Lake Temple, I have gradually become increasingly aware that many of God's children take too many serious Gospel principles and covenants for granted. We hear sacred teachings which are pleasing to our spirits. We witness miracles which touch our souls. We learn eternal truths which result in varying levels of motivations in our lives.

Why are we not more responsive to such powerful and great opportunities? Perhaps, like the Nephites of old, we too will have to personally hear the voice of the Father three times before we truly will listen and hear.

How sad that is! We, who have been given so much in these last days, seem to use so little. I believe that one of the reasons for this is that we look for the obvious, the plain, the readily-available. To truly capitalize on all that God has bestowed upon us, we must extend and enlarge our combined physical and spiritual visions.

We must teach ourselves to see the whole plan of our Heavenly Father. To become absorbed in relatively unimportant details is to lose the Spirit of extensive understanding. To focus entirely on today's tasks and tomorrow's problems is to lose sight of our ultimate potential as God's sons and daughters.

It is my personal prayer that this publication will assist you in accomplishing your fullest potential as you keep your whole focus on God's entire plan for the human race in general and yourself in particular.

Acknowledgments

One frequent statement that is often heard is that no man is an island unto himself. How true that statement is!

Serving as a missionary couple opens up your vision to a number of the realities of life. One of these for me personally is to realize the blessings of having a most sensitive companion who helps me stay on course. Rosa has been, and continues to be, of tremendous assistance in gathering, synthesizing, and organizing the material used in this publication. In addition to her sweet, faithful prayers, which do find access to Heavenly Father, she has been a source of continuing inspiration and enthusiastic motivation.

Our daughter, Betty, has also devoted much time and a great deal of energy to organizing the program in the word processer, and in teaching me how to use it. Her professional instincts, talents, and training have resulted in many valuable suggestions for developing, improving, and organizing the material.

Special thanks are also offered to Michael Bennett who computerized some of the graphics, and to Donna Gordon,

Bob and Linda Hadley, Norma Lewis, and Audrey Schultze all of whom served as editors. As Bovee once said: *"The small courtesies sweeten life; the greater enable it."* Our lives have truly been enriched by the willingness of these wonderful people to help improve this publication.

Introduction

On 31 October 1838, the Prophet Joseph Smith and several of his associates were arrested at Far West, Missouri. This act occurred as a result of a betrayal four days after Governor Lilburn W. Boggs issued his infamous extermination order against the Church and its members.

For the next several weeks, these church leaders were abused and insulted. They were forced to march to Independence and then to Richmond. By 30 November 1838, they were housed in the Liberty Jail unconvicted of any crime.

The Prophet and his friends suffered tremendously. There were many incidences of inhumane treatment, insufficient food, poisoned meals, no sleeping quarters, and restricted contact with the outside world. They were forced always to rest on straw placed on hard plank and stone floors.

During all of this time, the members of the Church were suffering heavy and constant persecution from violent mobs. They truly needed their Prophet's leadership in those desperate hours. Between 20 March and 25 March 1839, the Prophet dictated a lengthy communication. President Joseph Fielding

Smith referred to this as one of the greatest letters ever written by man as a result of the humblest of inspiration. He further stated that none other but a noble soul who was filled with the spirit of the true love of Christ could possibly have ever written such a letter.

Sections 121, 122, and 123 of the Doctrine and Covenants were extracted from this communication as written by the Prophet Joseph Smith. These sections are officially approved as revelations to the Church from the Lord, thus testifying to the Divine inspiration received by the Prophet when he penned the letter.

This collection of thoughts is offered under the umbrella of several key verses of Section 121. Some of these thoughts have been previously presented to the missionaries of the South Carolina Columbia Mission in the form of printed booklets, zone conference talks, and General Authority addresses to the missionaries as they conducted mission tours with us.

You see, the suffering and the searching and the need to serve the Lord is not yet finished. Each of us must endure the "refiner's fire" so that we can become purified and worthy to be exalted in the presence of the Father and the Son and the Holy Ghost. This refiner's fire can be referred to as your Zion's Camp.

In order to accomplish this, we must suffer and search and serve. Perhaps this publication may help you to accomplish your task. Even for the Prophet, the Liberty Jail experiences were not enough. He was still to seal his work and his testimony with his blood.

There is a price to be paid for exaltation. Are you willing and ready to pay it? A basic truism is that it isn't just going to happen. Victories are won before the battles. They are won, before they are fought, in the planning, preparation, training, and discipline of all those who are involved. It is up to us to plan, to prepare ourselves, and to develop self-discipline - all like unto the Savior. Now is the time to prepare for our ultimate victory - Exaltation in the Celestial Kingdom.

One special note is worthy of emphasis. As you study each chapter, you will become very aware of the fact that a number of key concepts are repeated several of times. Such concepts include, but are not limited to, repentance, obedience, temple covenants, personal righteousness, and faithful service.

Elder Ezra Taft Benson said that "....*repetition is the key to learning....*" [we] "*need to hear the truth repeated, especially because there is so much falsehood abroad*" (see *The Teachings of Ezra Taft Benson*, p. 305). Therefore, it is my humble prayer that you will see the value of my use of repetition. My extensive Church and public school experiences tell me that the most critical truths need to be heard over and over again before we begin to open our eyes and create success in our lives in the Gospel plan.

Definitions

Several words have been used frequently in this publication. Therefore, the following definitions are offered to help with your understanding of them.

EXALTATION - *a place rather than a condition or a state.* It is the highest degree in the Celestial Kingdom - the ultimate reward offered by the Godhead for faithful, obedient service sealed by the Holy Spirit of Promise.

INTERDEPENDENCE - *the most interactive of all human relationships.* It includes the selfless aspects of dependence and independence and lifts them into higher levels of motivation. An interdependent person is one whose motives are pure and who is devoid of guile and hypocrisy.

PROACTIVE - *the state of daily living in which a person takes complete charge of his or her life, even though family life is involved.* The opposite of this is to be reactive in which condition a person takes life as it comes and lets it just happen. Proactive people feel that they are responsible for their own actions in life, and they actively seek to establish and maintain full control over those actions.

WIN-WIN - *situations in which all participants in a given situation emerge with personal victories.* Habitual losing in life results in poor self-image, low self-esteem, and lack of self-confidence. Winning comes from proactive interdependence in which persons win regularly, but not at the expense of others.

Chapter One

O GOD, WHERE ART THOU?

D&C 121:1 — "O God, where art thou? And where is the pavilion that covereth thy hiding place?"

O God, where art thou? What a beautifully startling question! In asking it, the Prophet Joseph Smith was already in possession of the answer to the question of *where*. He wanted to know *when*. His real concern was when would the Lord provide relief for the persecuted members of His true Church.

The Savior has not made any secret of His whereabouts. His open invitation to all is to *"come unto me."* It is man who hides Him in mysticism and philosophy. Perhaps the plain truth is too simplistic for many to comprehend or accept. As a result, we have substantial differences in who He is, where He is, and even what He is.

Today, many people are still trying to find out where the Savior is. Some think they know because they confess His name. Millions of others are searching in a vast variety of philosophies, religions, writings, and events which seem to be "hiding places" for Christ.

For example, missionaries were teaching a lady who had been raised in a religion that believes the three—in—one concept of the Godhead. She had a cross that showed Christ in

2   Where Art Thou

the center of it. She accepted most of the teachings of the
missionaries but had difficulty with our belief of the three
separate and distinct beings in the Holy Trinity. After much
praying, both with the missionaries and on her own, she was
given a vision of that cross but, all through her dream, there
were three separate and distinct personages on it. She knew
then that her previous belief was not true.

One Indian tribe in America believes in an all—wise
personage who stands behind "The First Man" and "The First
Woman." This all—wise personage is generally spoken of as
a "Man" who is supreme. Working with him is his son, who
is consistently spoken of as "the man who never died."
Associated with these two individuals is a messenger —
"someone who is able to talk to the people."

Millions of people on earth today follow the teachings of
individuals such as Confucious, Buddha, Mohammed, and
Moses. Those who worship as Christians are numerically in
the minority of the world's population today. Those who
worship a Holy Trinity composed of three separate and
distinct Gods are even more so. It would also be safe to say that
a number of those who worship this latter concept often do not
fully understand the characteristics and attributes of the Gods
who comprise the Holy Trinity.

The Apostle Paul realized how true this was of the Jews
who had crucified the Christ for whom they had been looking
but failed to recognize when He came. He wrote " . . .*when
they knew God, they glorified him not as God, neither were
thankful; but became vain in their imaginations, and their
foolish heart was darkened. Professing themselves to be wise,
they became fools, and changed the glory of the uncorruptible
God into an image made like to corruptible man, and to birds,
and fourfooted beasts, and creeping things. Wherefore God
also gave them up to uncleanness through the lusts of their
own hearts, to dishonor their own bodies between themselves:*

Chapter 1   3

who changed the truth of God into a lie, and worshipped and served the creature more than the Creator, who is blessed for ever . . . " (see Romans 1:21—25).

In Matthew 13:5—6, we read: *"Some [seeds] fell upon stony places, where they had not much earth: and forthwith they sprung up, because they had no deepness of earth:". . ."and because they had no root, they withered away."* Too many people are exactly like these seeds. They are not well—grounded or rooted in the concept of the Godhead as it was taught to Father Adam and so we have all kinds of theories about that concept. On the other hand, people who are well—grounded in the Gospel should have a deep and extensive root system stemming from the true knowledge of the Godhead and extending into every phase of their existence giving nourishment for every need.

What about you? Do you truly know the Lord Jesus Christ? Do you fully comprehend your *role* and *position* in His great mission? Are you searching for Him in the right ways — through *study, prayer,* and *service*? Have you inwardly committed yourself to total and unquestioning *obedience* and *consecration*? Are you really willing to pay the *price asked* of you by the Savior no matter what it is?

In this world of rapid living, vast technological advantages, and handy comfort, it is too easy to lose sight of very basic spiritual concepts. We want, and can receive, ready answers to many of our questions. If such quick replies are not forthcoming, we lose interest, even to the eternal questions of Who are we?; Why are we here?; and Where are we going? Generally, man wants to know now. If he is unable or unwilling to wait, he invents something that pacifies him, even if he loses sight of the real truth.

All of us are born for a reason. Unfortunately, all of us do not take the time or make the effort to discover why. We tend

4   Where Art Thou

to accept our birth as a fact of life over which we had no control
and then we go from that point forward somewhat blindly. Is
it any wonder then that we think God is lost?

Compare that attitude with what two of our leaders have stated:

*"You, my young brothers and sisters, were sent to
earth through royal lineage. You were provided with a
fulness of truth so that you would not be blinded by the
sophistries of men or of devils. You young men were
given the priesthood which empowers you to be a rep-
resentative of Jesus Christ. You young sisters will be
blessed to bear sons and daughters and bring them
through the veil to mortality. You were chosen to come
here when the gospel is on the earth, and during a time
when events are building up toward the return of Jesus
Christ"* (see *Teachings of Ezra Taft Benson*, pp. 556—7).

*"The Lord has chosen a small number of choice spirits of
sons and daughters out of all the creations of God, who are to
inherit this earth; and this company of choice spirits have
been kept in the spirit world for six thousand years to come
forth in the last days to stand in the flesh in this last dispensation of the fulness of times, to organize the kingdom of God
upon the earth, to build it up, and to defend it and to receive
the eternal and everlasting priesthood"* (see President Wilford
Woodruff, *Title of Liberty*, p. 197).

Does this sound as if we have lost Jesus or that He has lost
us? Such prophetic words are true. Abraham recorded that
God stood in the midst of the noble and great souls and said
that He would make them His rulers. He included Abraham in
that group and told him that he (Abraham) was chosen before
he was born (see Abraham 3:22—23).

Lest you interpret that scripture too narrowly, you must
remember that you were included in that group of noble and

Chapter 1   5

great souls, just as the two Church leaders quoted above stated. For additional evidence of your greatness, study and ponder the truths written by Alma in Chapter 13, verse 3: *"And this is the manner after which they* [you] *were ordained — being called and prepared from the foundation of the world according to the foreknowledge of God, on account of their* [your] *exceeding faith and good works; in the first place being left to choose good or evil; therefore they* [you] *having chosen good, and exercising exceedingly great faith, are called with a holy calling, yea, with that holy calling which was prepared with, and according to, a preparatory redemption for such."*

In order for you to have been numbered amongst those potential spiritual giants whom the Lord saved for six thousand years to help establish the kingdom in this final dispensation, you must have demonstrated exceeding faith, performed good works, and chosen good over evil. Further, you must have been exceptionally stronger in such performances than many, many others. Thus, you were reserved by the Savior to come forth in this period of time. Are you personally convinced of this? Can you testify of it? If you can, does this sound as if Christ is lost in His pavilions?

Having accomplished such a high level of performance once, is there any reason why you cannot repeat it here on earth? You are the same spirit. Yes, you have forgotten all, but you have an earthly body to help you if you can and will "spiritualize" it. And you have living prophets, beautiful scriptures, personal revelation, meaningful temple ordinances and instruction, the companionship of the Holy Ghost, and the power and authority of the Priesthood to assist you in your righteous desires to find Christ.

But, be careful. Do not adopt a "better than they" attitude. Remember that great lesson taught to us by

6   Where Art Thou

Ammon who had been instrumental in helping thousands
of Lamanites to see the marvelous light of God. When
Aaron, his brother, rebuked him for seemingly boasting,
Ammon replied: *" . . . I do not boast in my own strength,
nor in my own wisdom; but behold, my joy is full, yea,
my heart is brim with joy, and I will rejoice in my God.
Yea, I know that I am nothing; as to my strength I am
weak; therefore I will not boast of my God, for in his
strength I can do all things; . . ." (Alma 26:11—12)*

In all of this, of course, we are opposed by Lucifer who is
the author of confusion, opposed to peace, and the perpetuator
of lies. He will attack us in our weakest habits and unguarded
behaviors. Most of the time he will engineer these attacks
through other people using misquoted scriptures, false philosophies, opportunities for self—indulgence, our poor self—
image, unrepented transgressions, rationalizations, and supposed opportunities to do good.

His battle plan is to cause us to question our own identity
and testimony, to raise doubts in our minds about "errors" in
the scriptures, revelations, and leaders, and to encourage us to
be intolerant, unkind, impatient, contentious, prideful, and a
prattler of gossip. Unfortunately, we get down on his level and
in his squalor. There is a part of us that seems to rejoice in such
negative behaviors. We even, on occasion, seem to enjoy
them. For example, how often have you repeated what you
know to be lies or gossip?

President Ezra Taft Benson assessed these conditions
when he wrote: *"The Lord has on the earth some potential spiritual giants whom He saved for some six
thousand years to help bear off the kingdom triumphantly
and the devil is trying to put them to sleep. The devil
knows that he probably won't be too successful in
getting them to commit many great and malignant sins
of commission. So he puts them into a deep sleep, like
Gulliver, while he strands them with little sins of*

Chapter 1

omission. And what good is a sleepy, neutralized, luke-warm giant as a leader? (see *The Teachings of Ezra Taft Benson*, p. 403)."

We must always be alert and on guard but not standing still on sentry duty. Luke told us that the kingdom of God is within us (see Luke 17:21). The Lord instructed us to look to Him in every one of our thoughts and to not doubt nor fear Him (see D&C 6:36). We are the crowning achievement in God's creations but we must continue to endure our "Zion's Camp" if we are to add to our great work in the pre—existence and be of superb value to the Lord in this phase of our existence.

> *"If thou canst plan a noble deed,*
> *And never flag till it succeed.*
> *Though in the strife thy heart shall bleed,*
> *Whatever obstacles control,*
> *Thine hour will come — go on, true soul!*
> *Thou'll win the prize, thou'll reach the goal."*
> (Charles Mackay)

"O God, where art thou?" With our divine heritage and with all of the help that God has provided for us, does that question exist in our minds? We have been given much. Much is therefore expected from us. But if we have questions as to where God is, who we are, and what is our final destination, we will never be able to maximize our potential nor will we see God clearly. He will always be hiding in pavilions from us as we erect excuses, rationalizations, and philosophies to blind our vision.

It is not God who is lost. It is our task to find Him and keep our relationships alive and strong every moment of every day, but we must be looking in the right direction, be doing the right things, and paying the full price, and following His example. The power of that example is beautifully recounted in a poem by Leona B. Gates.

"IN HIS STEPS"

"The road is rough, I said
Dear Lord, there are stones that hurt me so
And He said, Dear child I understand
I walked it long ago.

But there is a cool green path, I said
Let me walk there a time.
No child, He gently answered me,
The green path does not climb.

My burden, I said, is far too great,
How can I bear it so?
My child, said He, I remember its weight,
I carried my cross, you know.

But I said, I wish there were friends with me
Who would make my way their own.
And so, I climbed the stony path,
Content at last to know,
That where my Savior had not gone
I would not need to go.

And strangely then I found new friends,
The burden grew less sore.
As I remembered — long ago
He went that way before."

Chapter Two

PEACE BE UNTO THY SOUL

D&C 121:7 — "My son, peace be unto thy soul; thine adversity and thine afflictions shall be but a small moment";

Peace be unto thy soul! What a beautiful condition to be in and how wonderful it would be to personally hear those words directed to you from the lips of the Savior Himself.

What would this require of us? How can we earn them? Earn them we must for there can be no eternal peace in the life of a member of this Church unless he or she is admitted into Exaltation in the Celestial Kingdom.

Why is this so? Because unto this were we ordained — nothing less. We know what we must do. The prophets have shown us the way. Jesus has established the requirements and has provided us with all that we need in this life to fulfil them. Alma told us that *" . . .this life is the time for men to prepare to meet God; yea, behold the day of this life is the day for men to perform their labors"* (see Alma 34:32).

With such clear instruction available to us, what is it that *prevents* us from achieving the type of peace spoken of above? The answer can be given in one word — **transgression**. This is not the only reason, but it far outweighs all others.

10   Where Art Thou

Moses fully understood this answer. He wrote: *"Where-fore teach it unto your children, that all men, everywhere, must repent, or they can in nowise inherit the kingdom of God, for no unclean thing can dwell there, or dwell in his presence; for, in the language of Adam, Man of Holiness is his name, and the name of his Only Begotten is the Son of Man, even Jesus Christ, a righteous Judge, who shall come in the meridian of time "* (see Moses 6:57).

In connection with transgression and repentance, there frequently appears to be a mental attitude amongst numerous individuals that little sins are all right and that Jesus in exercising His great love for each of us would most certainly overlook small transgressions. Such a concept is in direct opposition to the beautiful and clear instruction given by Amulek when he contended with Zeezrom: *"And I say unto you again that he [God] cannot save them in their sins; for I cannot deny his word, and he hath said that no unclean thing can inherit the kingdom of heaven; therefore, how can ye be saved, except ye inherit the kingdom of heaven. Therefore, ye cannot be saved in your sins"* (see Alma 11:37).

Zeezrom never could quite grasp that. He had difficulty in separating the words "in" and "from". Jesus cannot possibly save us in our sins. The Law of Justice totally prevents that. Eternal law also prevents that. What the Savior can do is to save us from our sins.

Given such knowledge, it becomes perfectly rational to say that to be clean means to fully repent of **every one** of our transgressions. This necessitates the implementation of the five steps of repentance in their fulness as outlined by Spencer W. Kimball in his great book *Miracle of Forgiveness* — a must reading for each member.

In a recent fireside at Brigham Young University, it was stated that repentance is not a free ride. It is not a simple expression of sorrow. It comes only with a personal price that

Chapter 1

involves suffering. It requires a broken heart and a contrite spirit. People who knowingly sin often expect that the burden of suffering will be fully born by Jesus Christ. Such is a false expectation because it does not solve the basic problem and because the Redeemer only paid for those sins of which we fully repent.

A person who sins is like a tree that bends easily in the wind. On a windy and rainy day the tree bends so deeply against the ground that the leaves become soiled with mud [sin]. If we only focus on cleaning the leaves, the weakness in the tree that allowed it to bend and soil its leaves may remain. Merely cleaning the leaves does not strengthen the tree. Similarly, a person who is simply sorry to be soiled by sin will transgress again in the next high wind.

On the other hand, some people feel that they have to be beaten over and over again before they have paid a big enough price for their sins. The Lord requires from us a godly sorrow. This means a sufficient penalty based on a fair price — nothing more, nothing less. You will know when you have paid a fair price by the feeling of utter peacefulness that enters your heart — a true sign that the Lord has completely forgiven you and remembers your sin no more.

If and when we effect a complete repentance, we will be changed from a weak person who once transgressed into a strong person with a spiritual stature that qualifies us to dwell in the presence of God. This is what Moses meant: *"For by the water ye keep the commandment; by the Spirit ye are justified, and by the blood ye are sanctified."* (see Moses 6:60).

On April 6, 1830 — the day The Church of Jesus Christ of Latter—Day Saints was organized, the Lord told the Prophet Joseph Smith: *"And we know that justification through the grace of our Lord and Savior Jesus Christ is just and true."* (see D&C 20:30).

Such instructions should remove all doubt from your mind

12   Where Art Thou

that the Law of Justification is essential to your becoming pure and obtaining for yourself the eternal peace of God. The clarity in these instructions also disputes the contention among the sects of the Christian world that men are justified by faith alone and that men are saved by grace alone.

It is worthy of note that the Lord always does things sequentially. Before giving this instruction to the Prophet, He had already restored the principle of baptism, the Gift of the Holy Ghost, and the Priesthood. Each of these combine to form a very basic ingredient in the Law of Justification and you cannot teach this law without all three. With the Lord, first things must come first.

The Law of Justification is the provision that a wise Redeemer has placed in the gospel to assure that no unrighteous performance [act] will be binding on earth and in heaven, and that no person will be able to add to his or her glory in the hereafter by gaining any unearned blessings.

This law is directly connected to the Law of Justice which requires us to pay the penalty for every transgression that we have committed in this life with the exception of those which we have truly repented of through the proper steps of repentance. In these cases, Jesus Christ mercifully paid those penalties by invoking the Law of Mercy.

The full and complete definition of the Law of Justification is: *"All covenants, contracts, bonds, obligations, oaths, vows, performances, connections, associations, or expectations, which you must abide in order to be saved and exalted must be entered into and performed in righteousness."* (see D&C 132:7) Then, the Holy Spirit will justify you for salvation in what you have done.

The key thing that you have to remember is that every act you do on the path to Exaltation must be ratified [sealed] by the Holy Spirit of Promise. This means that *all* of your deeds must be approved by the Holy Ghost. If there are any for which you have

Chapter 1   13

not truly paid the price of full and complete repentance, you will be required to suffer even as Jesus did (see D&C 19:16—17).

Since no unclean thing can enter Exaltation, then all transgressions must be cleansed from your soul. It is axiomatic that our suffering must always be in direct proportion to the sin. Thus, the greater the sin, the greater the suffering. How can you ensure adequate payment? There will be absolutely no question if you explicitly follow the steps detailed by Spencer W. Kimball.

As with all other doctrines of salvation, the Law of Justification is available because of the loving, atoning sacrifice of the Savior. It becomes operative in your life for your good on the conditions of personal righteousness — those that will be described in the next chapter on sanctification. When justification and sanctification exist together in your soul, you will be in a position to hear the Savior say: *"My son* [daughter] *peace be unto thy soul."*

The two saddest words in any language are **"IF ONLY."** Yet, in reality, they do not change a thing. They keep you facing the wrong way. They waste time. They become an excuse for not trying. They lead you along the path to the eternal loss of blessings and family. There is no peace in **"IF ONLY."**

This concept is critically important because we are faced with a decision every time we make a covenant, are taught a commandment, or make a resolve to change. We basically have two choices. One comes if we receive the instruction or covenant positively and obey it completely. We then receive the accompanying blessings and we are entitled to the full sanctifying blessings promised by the Lord. This enables us to become more Christ—like in our attributes and, as we do, we come to know God. *"For how knoweth a man the master whom he has not served . . ."* (see Mosiah 5:13).

The following diagram graphically illustrates our choices as we receive commandments from the Lord.

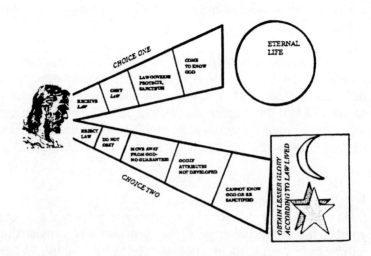

Choice one is the upward path. Choice two is the alternative. Our wise Heavenly Father always gives us two choices — otherwise, He could have appointed Lucifer to bring us back into His presence rather than Jesus Christ.

The second choice leads us in the opposite direction as outlined above. The only way we can move from choice two to choice one is through the process of repentance. After repenting sufficiently far enough to feel more justified in Christ, we usually rebuke ourselves with an *"If only, I had _____."*

It is possible to embark on choice one, then fall down to choice two. This always involves transgressions, many of which are rooted in *"If only _____"* types of rationalizations — a very favorite weapon in Lucifer's arsenal of temptations. Rationalizations lead only one way — down.

The one step in the repentance process that often appears to be the hardest to achieve is that of restitution. It is impossible to give back or restore some things such as chastity. There are many reasons why restitution may be extremely difficult but nevertheless you must try to accomplish the best you can. No one asks you to destroy yourself or your family

Chapter 1   15

in the process so think through the situation prayerfully; then do the best you can. That is all the Lord asks. He is an exact task master but not a unreasonably hard one.

Another favorite tool of Satan is discouragement which frequently comes upon us when the task of overcoming all of our sins looks to be insurmountable. Yet even the longest journey must begin with the first step and every journey is made easier by goal setting. The surest way to eat an elephant is one planned bite after another planned bite.

Our overall goal is to *"be even as He is."* (see 3 Nephi 27:27). No one could possibly even think of attaining that overall goal unless smaller goals are developed. Brigham Young taught: *"I will put my own definition to the term 'sanctification' and say it consists in overcoming **every sin** and bringing all into subjection to the law of Christ."*

The drive to overcome sin is rooted in our value system. If we see nothing wrong in what we have done, or are doing, we will not repent. Because of this condition, we frequently have to re—examine our values before we develop the desire to repent. It is quite often the case that, if we change our values, we find that our motivation to repent is greatly enhanced.

Hyrum W. Smith uses this illustration to encourage us to look deeply at our value system. Suppose you are standing on the top of a three hundred foot high building, and that there is a hundred foot separation between that building and a similar one opposite you. Suppose, further, that the only way to cross from where you are standing to the building opposite you is by walking on a four—inch wide I—beam that bridges the gap between the two buildings.

The question asked by Hyrum W. Smith is: "What would you cross the I—beam for?" Would money entice you? Would you consider it if it meant saving your mother, or some other loved one, from certain death? Would you cross it if the Savior

16   Where Art Thou

was standing there with outstretched arms beckoning to you?

To answer those types of questions becomes a real challenge of your entire system of values. It raises profound inquiries not only as to your motives but also as to your goals for achieving those motives. The question: "What would I cross the I—beam for?" also challenges your desire to change inappropriate goals and motives.

Every accountable person needs to set short and long range goals. The best way to accomplish this is to take an inventory of yourself, your attitudes, and your areas of needed improvements. An excellent format for such an inventory is provided for you in the next chapter.

Once you complete the inventory, make a list of the attributes you need to change. Determine if repentance is necessary. If so, take care of it first. Then prioritize your list. Go to work first on the one that is the easiest to achieve. This will do wonders for your self—image and confidence as well as providing motivation to continue. Success breeds success. Moreover, those attributes which you rated as hardest strangely enough move up the list and eventually become easier to achieve.

Discouragement and rationalization will most certainly result, but you must not let Satan's tools stop you. Once in a while, step back from the forest so that you can ascertain if you are still heading in your pre—determined direction on the right path. If you encounter problems, take another look at your sub—goals and re—evaluate your priorities.

Do not waste time in regretting the fact that you were not able to achieve all of your sub—goals yesterday. Each new day brings you another chance. You may have underestimated the time you needed. You may have misjudged the effort the task required. You may have encountered unanticipated interference from someone or something over which you had no control.

Chapter 1   17

Every time you take one more step towards complete justification, Satan will do everything he can to encourage you to take two steps backward. At such times, remember Elder Paul H. Dunn's classic: *"It is not how many times you get knocked down that counts, it is how many times you pick yourself up that proves your strength of character."*

As President Spencer W. Kimball has made famous: **"DO IT."** Add to that and say: **"DO IT — BECOME JUSTIFIED, THEN SANCTIFIED — NOW."**

18   Where Art Thou

Chapter Three

ENDURE IT WELL

D&C 121:8 — "And then, if thou endure it well, God shall exalt thee on high; thou shalt triumph over all thy foes."

Because no unclean thing can dwell in the presence of God and because God dwells in Exaltation, it naturally follows that if God will exalt us on high, we must become clean first. In this important context, cleanliness is synonymous with purity.

"Blessed are the pure in heart; for they shall see God" (see Matthew 5:8). To be pure is to be completely clean, to be free from what weakens, and to be free from fault or guilt. Such a condition is not based on what we have accomplished but rather it is predicated on what we are becoming — like unto Christ.

Elder Dallin H. Oaks stated that to become pure is a process. It is the result of more than our actions. It is also the result of our attitudes, our motives, and our desires — each of which is an ingredient in a pure heart. He suggested four steps in purifying our lives.

1. Face up to our imperfections and the need to repent (see Chapter Two, page 9—15).

2. Begin by questioning yourself — strip away pretenses

and false fronts.

3. Examine your attitudes and become positive and proactive.

4. Control your thoughts (see Chapter Ten, pp. 106—108).

In regard to the second point made by Elder Oaks, we need to consider a few additional thoughts. Too often in dealing with people, even those very close to us, we get caught up in pretenses and false fronts. They loom very large in our human relationships. In reality, however, they are often only symptoms of the real problem and not the problem itself. If we waste time dealing with symptoms, we seldom ever will identify and resolve the problem.

For example, if you go to a doctor complaining of several symptoms, he could very easily misdiagnose the problem, operate on the wrong part of the body, and cause you many more troubles. Normally, a doctor would run more tests designed to isolate the cause of your pain in order to be sure of how to help you.

This analogy is helpful in dealing with others. People build up all kinds of pretenses and false fronts — sometimes referred to as "walls" — such as anger, hostility, sarcasm, untimely humor, withdrawal, silence, lack of communication, tears, and many, many others. Like the doctor, we must "look past" these and strive diligently to understand the real problem. Only then can we be of help. We must specifically do it for ourselves as well, although we may need empathic listening from someone we trust in order to accomplish it.

Our Savior is not asking us to do the impossible. He has shown us the way and has established the pattern and it was not easy for him. *"For this is thankworthy, if a man for conscience toward God endure grief, suffering wrongfully. For what glory is it, if, when ye be buffeted for your faults, ye shall take*

Chapter 1   21

it patiently? but if, when ye do well, and suffer for it, ye take it patiently, this is acceptable with God. For even hereunto were ye called: because Christ also suffered for us, leaving us an example, that ye should follow his steps" (see 1 Peter 2:19—21).

Why would Jesus suffer for us if there were no chance for us to become pure? The answer, of course, is that, as a result of His suffering, He can offer us the opportunity to become justified and sanctified. *"And we know also, that sanctification through the grace of our Lord and Savior Jesus Christ is just and true, to all those who love and serve God with all their mights, minds, and strength"* (see D&C 20:31).

Exactly what does sanctification mean? It means to become clean, pure, and spotless before God. It means to be free from the blood and the sins of this world. It means to become a new creature of the Holy Ghost because your body has been renewed by the rebirth of the Spirit.

The condition of sanctification can be attained only by complete obedience to the laws, ordinances, and covenants of the Gospel. If we have transgressed any of these, we must have repented fully and properly (the Law of Justification). Thus, it is the Plan of Salvation which provides the system as well as the means whereby we can sanctify our soul in order to become a worthy candidate for Exaltation in the Celestial Kingdom.

Therefore, sanctification is a basic doctrine of Christ's teachings because it involves the Laws of Repentance, Justice, and Mercy. It also involves all other commandments. The time will come when the sanctified person will stand before the judgment bar of Jesus Christ and he or she will be spotless — free from all sin and transgression. It follows that the inevitable reward will be Exaltation!

The truthfulness of these thoughts are beautifully verified by Moroni. *"Yea, come unto Christ, and be perfected in him, and deny yourself of all ungodliness; and if ye shall deny*

22 Where Art Thou

yourselves of all ungodliness, and love God with all your might, mind and strength, then is his grace sufficient for you, that by his grace ye may be perfect in Christ; and if by the grace of God ye are perfect in Christ, ye can in nowise deny the power of God" (see Moroni 10:32).

In accordance with this scripture, if we are to come unto Christ and be perfected (sanctified) in Him, we must accomplish it by denying ourselves of all ungodliness. This provides the proof that we love God with all our might, mind, and strength and can never deny the power of God in our lives.

The burning question is now: Can such a condition be attained in this life? The answer is a very powerful yes! In fact, the Lord expects it of each of us and has so commanded us to accomplish it. *"Therefore, sanctify yourselves that your minds become single to God, and the days will come that you shall see him; for he will unveil his face unto you, and it shall be in his own time, and in his own way, and according to his own will"* (see D&C 88:68).

Once attained, where does sanctification lead us? Again, the Master provides the answer. *"That bodies who are of the celestial kingdom may possess it forever and ever; for, for this intent was it made and created, and for this intent are they sanctified. And they who are not sanctified through the law which I have given unto you, even the law of Christ, must inherit another kingdom, even that of a terrestrial kingdom, or that of a telestial kingdom"* (see D&C 88:20—21).

Inasmuch as sanctification is such a sweet and desirable status to achieve, what must we do to attain it? There are ten important steps.

1. **IMMERSION** — To attain sanctification we must become so immersed in living all of the teachings of the gospel of Jesus Christ that our thoughts and actions become pure and holy. We must yield hearts completely and unconditionally to God. We must be immersed as spiritually in living our

covenants as we were physically in the waters of baptism. Some are willing to consecrate themselves up to their knees or waists. Christ requires us to give as much as He gave — all.

2. **SINGLEMINDEDNESS** — Keeping our minds centered on Jesus Christ is the primary way to achieve this process of sanctification. He must become the very center of our thoughts and actions. Such singlemindedness means walking uprightly before God and seeking His divine will through study, prayer, and service. It means overcoming the natural man as outlined in Mosiah, Chapter 3 and becoming the spiritual man as described in Alma, Chapter 5 (see also Chapter Six of this publication). This can only be achieved if we immerse our lives in our temple covenants and unreservedly consecrate all that we are and all that we have to the single purpose of building up the Kingdom of God on earth. To begin such a mind set, you must convince yourself that you are a son or daughter of a very loving Father in Heaven and that you are of great importance to the work of Jesus Christ (see Abraham 3:22, Alma 13:3, and Chapter One).

3. **OBEDIENCE** — Obedience is the first law of the Kingdom of God. It is the first evidence to our Savior that we really do love Him, that we are worthy to represent Him here on earth, and that He can trust us not to blow in any direction in any breeze. *"And we will prove them herewith, to see if they will do all things whatsoever the Lord their God shall command them"* (see Abraham 3:25). Our desire to be a truly obedient servant of Jesus Christ can only find root in our undivided love for Him. We must eliminate our selfish tendencies, our fear of and for man, our desire for leadership positions, and our search for personal gain. We must thoroughly convince ourselves that all that we have, hope to have, are, or hope to become will only be achieved as a result of unquestioned obedience to God. Thus, we will be in the state described by the Prophet Joseph Smith: *"The nearer we approach perfection, the clearer our views become and the greater is our enjoyment, till we have overcome all the evils in*

24   Where Art Thou

*our lives and we have lost every desire for sin. Then, we will
be wrapped in the power and glory of our Maker and be caught
up to dwell with Him"* (see History of the Church 2:8).

4. **FAITH** — Exercising faith and producing good works
will permit us to know the mysteries of God and open our
minds to many of the truths shown to ancient prophets but
which they were commanded not to write (see Alma 26:22).
Do not, however, focus on the mysteries, for if you do you will
lose your testimony of the basics without which you cannot
ever hope to learn more. As the basic truths are revealed to
you, and, as you apply those basic truths in your daily living,
your faith turns to knowledge which generates more faith
projected into what was previously a mystery to you (see
Alma 32:18,21,26,34 and Moroni 10:4). The achievement of
this depth of faith is based on four factors, all of which must
be present in your life.

*A knowledge that Jesus Christ lives.

*A true understanding of His character, attributes, and mission.

*A willingness to sacrifice and consecrate all that you
have to the Savior.

*A total commitment to put off the natural man and his
weaknesses. Joseph Smith stated that a religion that does not
require the sacrifice [and consecration] of all things never has
sufficient power to produce all the faith [and knowledge]
necessary to lead you unto life and salvation in Exaltation.
When we have offered in sacrifice all that we have for truth's
sake, even our lives if necessary, God will accept our offering
and reward it with eternal life (see Lectures on Faith).

5. **REPENTANCE** — Without apology, Nephi tells it
like it is: *"...the kingdom of God is not filthy, and there cannot
be any unclean thing enter into the kingdom of God..."* (see
1 Nephi 15:34). While this step is covered in Chapter Two

Chapter 1   25

under the topic of "Justification," a few additional thoughts are necessary here. To be clean in the Lord's terms means total cleanliness — outward and inward — appearance, speech, thoughts, actions, and living areas. You must literally surround yourself with the type of cleanliness that eliminates all hypocrisy and which is congruent with your temple covenants. The all—seeing eye of God prevents us from hiding or covering up unrepented sins. Just because there is sin in the world, it does not mean that we have to be involved in it. All personal transgressions must be removed from your life and **only you can do that task**. When you overcome each sin through using the proper steps, Jesus is ready to forgive you and He will "...*remember them no more...*" (see D&C 58:42). The sweetest and most peaceful feeling in this world is to know that you have received His forgiveness. The reward is to receive eternal life (see D&C 133:62).

6. **HUMILITY** — The personal promise of the Savior for those who are humble is that "...*he that shall humble himself shall be exalted*" (see Matthew 23:12). The deepest possible state of humility that we can reach is to possess a full recognition and acceptance of our true relationship to God. When you have achieved this status, you will find that you have also deepened many of the other attributes of Jesus Christ (see Chapter Thirteen) and you are solidly on the road to your overall goal — to be as He is — sanctified.

To acquire and maintain this depth of humility you must follow steps 1, 2, 3, 4, and 5 above in that order. In addition, you must intensify your fasting and praying. Fast for a purpose. Open and close each fast with a prayer for that specific purpose. Remember the counsel of Alma in all of your righteous desires: "...*they had given themselves to much prayer, and fasting; therefore they had the spirit of prophecy, and the spirit of revelation, and when they taught, they taught with power and authority of God*" (see Alma 17:3). Attaining humility in the Lord will give you many blessings (see Mosiah 27:22—23) and your testimony will be added upon (see Alma 5:46). This attainment is recognizable when you can reply as

26   Where Art Thou

Alma did: *"...Believest thou in Jesus Christ, who shall come? And he said: Yea, I believe all the words which thou has spoken"* (see Alma 45:4—5).

In order to know all the words, you must study diligently. You cannot live nor teach what you do not know and understand. Studying brings knowledge; knowledge brings wisdom; wisdom brings obedience and patience which in turn brings love and humility in Christ Jesus.

7. **LOVE** — *"If thou lovest me thou shalt serve me and keep **all** my commandments"* (see D&C 42:29). Note how the Lord prefaces this scripture with *"if thou lovest me"* — a question. He follows this with two conditions: to serve and to keep all of His commandments. Obviously, the highest manifestation of love on your part can only be seen if you fulfil these two conditions. It is therefore logical to conclude that serving others and obedience to God's commandments combine to show our love of God and our love of God must combine serving and being obedient. You cannot have one without the other. Love has always been associated with and manifested through service because love is an active process and not a destination.

" ...Thou shalt love the Lord thy God with all thy heart, with all thy might, mind, and strength; and in the name of Jesus Christ thou shall serve him. Thou shalt love thy neighbor as thyself..." (see D&C 59:5—6).

Thus, love is a divine element in daily living. In and of itself, it represents our perfect relationship with each member of the Godhead as well as with our families, friends, and daily activities. Love must become an active and proactive force in our lives. Did not Christ give His life in love for each of us? Can our love for Him be of a lesser quality?

8. **REVELATION** — The scriptures are the revealed

Chapter 1   27

word of God. Because that is true, the principle of ongoing and continuous revelation is also true. This applies to that received for the Church through our living Prophet and that which you receive on a personal basis. As a child of God and as a servant of Jesus Christ, you are entitled to receive personalized revelation as often as needed, if you are worthy.

"And ye are to be taught from on high. Sanctify yourselves and ye shall be endowed with power, that ye may give even as I have spoken" (see D&C 43:16). To be taught from on high means that you will be led, guided, protected, and inspired through the Holy Ghost as the Savior decides. If you desire this, you are invited to develop and use the teaching principle often used by Elder Vaughn J. Featherstone. The first words out of his mouth, when he visits with a stake president at the opening session of his stake conference assignment, are: "President, I am here to fill your spiritual 'bucket'." He then proceeds to do it in all his teachings.

The following suggestions may help you to also use this concept:

*keep your spiritual "bucket" full through study, prayer, fasting, and service.

*believe without a doubt that God will speak to you.

*ask without fear for personal revelation.

*recognize when you are receiving personal revelation. Authenticate it through the Holy Ghost.

*live worthy to receive constant revelation for yourself.

*express appreciation constantly to God for such blessings and give Him the credit for your achievements.

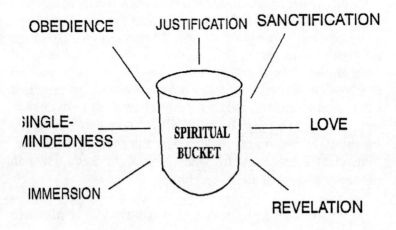

9. **SERVICE** — Even though discussed in Step 7, this subject needs further emphasis. *" . . .Choose you this day whom ye will serve"; . . ."but as for me and my house, we will serve the Lord"* (see Joshua 24:15). Contrary to the world's popular opinion, there is not a "grey area" between what is right and what is wrong. You can only serve God or Satan. You cannot serve both. The Lord said you cannot serve two masters (see Matthew 6:24). In addition, we are informed that *" . . .because thou are lukewarm, and neither cold nor hot, I will spue thee out of my mouth"* (see Revelation 3:16).

Chapter 1   29

As members of the Church, we have already put our hands to the plow. We have been and continue to be greatly blessed. We have been given more than any other people have ever been given to help us. For all of this, the Master asks us to serve Him with all of our heart, might, mind, and strength (see D&C 4).

Service to God is the foundation for personal peace and directional righteousness in this life and for Exaltation in the Celestial Kingdom. When you add righteous, selfless service to unrestricted love you get charity. Christ—like service should be based on and have root in love as demonstrated in the Parable of the Good Samaritan. When put together, you possess the pure love of Christ which is charity and it will endure forever (see Moroni 7:44—47). As Paul testified *"Who shall separate us from the love of Christ?" . . ."Nor height, nor depth, nor any other creature, shall be able to separate us from the love of God, which is in Christ Jesus our Lord"* (see Romans 8:35,39).

10. **TRIALS AND ADVERSITIES** — We all have been taught since birth that we came to earth to be tried and tested in order to prove ourselves worthy. The Lord told us that *" . . .all these things shall give you experience, and shall be for thy good"* (see D&C 122:7). Further, He informed President Brigham Young that *"My people must be tried in all things, that they may be prepared to receive the glory which I have prepared for them, even the glory of Zion; and he that will not bear chastisement is not worthy of the kingdom"* (see D&C 136:31).

Even so, despite our ready acceptance of this gospel principle, whenever trials and adversities come into our personal lives, we tend to be negative and move further *away* from the Lord. At such times, we should move *towards* Him for we need *His* help in working our way through and overcoming our problems. We teach the need for trials and adversities but we seem to expect that they should be visited upon everyone else. When we have them, we feel we are being punished by the Lord and that, since we are trying to live our religion, we should be therefore immune from too many problems. Hence, we react negatively to the Lord.

President Spencer W. Kimball told the story of a ship stranded off the coast of South America. The captain signalled to a passing ship to share their water with his passengers who were suffering from thirst. The passing vessel signalled back telling him to let down his bucket into the water in which they were floundering because they were in the mouth of the Amazon River where the water was fresh.

We frequently find it easy to become lost in our own trials and adversities by feeling sorry for ourselves and doubting the Lord's love for us. When this happens, we tend to lose the Holy Spirit. We must reverse that process. Instead of drawing away from God, we must look upon such trials and adversities as opportunities to grow in our weaknesses and we must use the powers of heaven even more in order to win these temporary battles.

There are a few critical concepts that we need to keep in proper perspective:

*Remember that the Lord will not try any one of us beyond our respective capacities to endure.

*Review your life to see if you are doing the right thing for the right reason. Give yourself humble credit for the good things you have done. One of the characteristics of individuals who have a poor self—image is the fact that they are very much unable to recognize success and to give themselves due credit. Hence, they are always "putting" themselves down.

*Purge yourself of all transgressions, even the little ones.

*Check your personal progress towards sanctification and exaltation.

Chapter 1   31

*Remember that you can only control your own life, not the lives of others. You probably waste significant time and energy worrying over events and people where you exercise no control.

*Ponder deeply your need to endure the refiner's fire if you are to emerge from this life as pure as gold in the eternity to come. You will find it much easier to accept life's problems if you ponder on this need in advance.

*Reflect on the fact that trials and adversities usually strike your weakest areas and by overcoming them you become stronger.

*Consider that all you endure is a part of your education in God's time. The Savior was sinless yet He endured much tribulation and finally death. Are you greater than He?

Think of the concept of the rubber band. It is of little use until it is stretched. It can be stretched quite a bit before it breaks. Stretch yourself as often and as far as you can in living the covenants and commandments. Then, when trials and adversities come, your "stretched" perspective will assist you in overcoming them so much easier.

In Chapter Thirteen, you will find an extensive discussion of those Christ—like attributes that we must achieve. After you have read, pondered, and understood them, prioritize them on a scale of one to ten, with ten being high. Your prioritization should be in ascending order of need. The lowest one will then be the attribute that you are the nearest to accomplishing in your life now. Put that list aside for a minute and look at the ten steps that we must use if we are to be sanctified. If there are any of these steps that you do not comprehend, go back and review them.

Look at the checklist below. If you had previously decided that the Christ—like attribute of "love" was the one you are

32   Where Art Thou

closest to achieving, then rate yourself on the ten steps towards sanctification using the attribute of "love." When you are finished, you will have come to the conclusion that you still need more work on "service," for example, in order to raise your attribute of "love" to the highest level possible. (Note that you must go to work on improving your strongest, not your weakest, area first. If you start on your weakest, you will soon suffer defeat and give up. By improving your strongest area first, you find instant success and you will make improvement in the remaining areas that much easier to achieve.)

This evaluation will help you set your personal goals for self—improvement in any Christ—like attribute on any phase of sanctification you wish to achieve. It will give you a very purposeful way of living the Gospel. Repeat your evaluation every month in order to determine your progress. The trend line should always be upwards. If you doubt your ability to honestly evaluate yourself, ask a close but trusted friend for confidential help.

CHRIST—LIKE ATTRIBUTE—SANCTIFICATION CHECKLIST

CHRIST-LIKE ATTRIBUTE:_____												
	Jan	Feb	Mar	Apr	May	Jun	Jul	Aug	Sep	Oct	Nov	Dec
IMMERSION												
SINGLE-MINDEDNESS												
OBEDIENCE												
FAITH												
REPENTANCE												
HUMILITY												
LOVE												
REVELATION												
SERVICE												
TRIALS & ADVERSITIES												

(Note: For each Attribute, rate yourself 1-10)

Chapter 1   33

If you thoroughly study the scriptures on sanctification, you will come to know that such an achievement is possible in this life. The closer you approach this objective, the more you must continue to abide the truth.

How will you know of your progress? The answer is in the oath and covenant of the priesthood, where it is stated, *"For whoso is faithful unto the obtaining these two priesthoods of which I have spoken, and the magnifying their calling, are sanctified by the Spirit unto the renewing of their bodies"* (see D&C 84:33).

Note the steps outlined by the Lord — obtain the priesthood, magnify the calling, sanctified by the Spirit, and renewing of the body. This is a **"feeling"** experience because as you do the first two steps you can **"feel"** the cleansing, purifying, and sanctifying power of the Holy Ghost. It is *real. You will know*. The fourth step of renewing your body will not be completely fulfilled until your resurrection — man or woman.

To help in this achievement, you should find a few suggestions useful.

*Strive to be in control of your life. Be proactive in seeking the loving care of the Savior. Make your life what you want it to be — sanctified. To be proactive is to make your life what you **want** it to be — to be in **complete charge** of your own life.

*Eliminate the influence of Satan from your life. The only power he can exert over you is that which you grant him. Our Heavenly Father placed enmity between Lucifer and the seed of Eve and, in so doing, gave each of us power to bruise (destroy) his works (see Moses 4:21 and Hebrews 2:14). Enmity means to hate, to oppose, or to be hostile to. It is shown in the Savior's injunction to hate the sin, but love the sinner.

*Look at each trial and adversity as a lesson to be learned — one that you need. After you have worked your way through it, re—assess to solidify that learning.

34   Where Art Thou

*Radiate the love and message of Jesus Christ in your face, your eyes, and your actions. Count your blessings often thus giving yourself an ever—deepening love of and for Him. The eyes are the window of the soul. Shakespeare said, *"They do not love that do not show love."*

*Edify everyone you meet. Impact upon them so positively that each will leave your presence feeling better for having been with you.

*Remember, and keep ever in the forefront of your thoughts, these two beautiful promises, *"And if your eye be single to my glory, your whole bodies shall be filled with light, and there shall be no darkness in you; and that body which is filled with light comprehendeth all things. Therefore, sanctify yourselves that your minds become single to God, and the days will come that you shall see him; for he will unveil his face unto you, and it shall be in his own time, and in his own way, and according to his own will"* (see D&C 88:67—68).

"And in that day that they shall exercise faith in me, saith the Lord, even as the brother of Jared did, that they may become sanctified in me, then will I manifest unto them the things which the brother of Jared saw, even to the unfolding unto them of all my revelations, saith Jesus Christ, the Son of God, and the Father of the heavens and of the earth, and all things that in them are" (see Ether 4:7).

IS THE REWARD WORTH THE SACRIFICE? ARE YOU WILLING TO PAY THE PRICE?

You are a child of God. You can be sanctified. However, you must always remember that sanctification is a **process**, not the ultimate goal. The goal is EXALTATION and there is at least one more part of that process that has to be completed, after you have approached sanctification, before we can reach the goal. That part is what is referred to as "Making Your Calling and Election Sure." We will therefore discuss this subject thoroughly in Chapter Fifteen.

Chapter Four

THOU ART NOT YET AS JOB

D&C 121:9—10 — "Thy friends do stand by thee, and they shall hail thee again with warm hearts and friendly hands. Thou art not yet as Job; thy friends do not contend against thee, neither charge thee with transgression, as they did Job."

The classic reference to Job in these two verses is best understood if we read a few more words about this great man. *"Behold, thou hast instructed many, and thou hast strengthened the weak hands. Thy words have upholden him that was falling, and thou has strengthened the feeble knees. But now it is come upon thee, and thou faintest; it toucheth thee, and thou art troubled. Is not this thy fear, thy confidence, thy hope, and the uprightness of thy ways?"* (see Job 4:3—6).

Such words are truer than we care to admit. Previous experiences tell us how easy it is to keep motivated in our labors when the sea is calm and the winds are still. But, as soon as an apparently "authoritative" person feeds us untruths, partial truths, or even gossip, how quickly we doubt, bend, falter, and question the truths we have always heard even from our youth. Some individuals experience an evaporation of their testimonies when faced with a Bible scholar's different but "believably plausible" interpretation of scriptures from the Old or New Testament.

Why should such a thing happen? How can a lifelong member who has constantly attended Church and even taken classes in Seminary and Institute lose a testimony so quickly and easily? After all, we have full access to the revealed scriptures from which to learn. We also have the Holy Ghost as our revealer of truth on as steady a basis as we desire. He will be our testifier of Christ's divinity and mission.

In addition to those two great blessings, we can pray for and receive confirmation of the various solutions which we work out to solve our problems. And, as if these were not enough, there are the temple ordinances which instruct us and the priesthood to give us solid direction in life. Yet even now the list is incomplete. There are living prophets to teach us in love and out of sincere concern for our welfare and eternal progress.

But even though we have these warm hearts and friendly hands and our friends do not contend against us, we seem to give up so readily and so easily when faced with challenges. We appear to want to fit the teachings of the Gospel into man's philosophies and scriptural interpretations and when the fit is not a good one, we doubt what we have been taught. In reality, we must never do that. We have to try to fit man's teachings into the Gospel and, if they do not fit, we must put them aside for a season or even discard them outright without even feeling poorly for having done it.

It is so strange that, in spite of all of man's wisdom, he cannot find satisfactory answers to two of life's most basic questions. They are: Who am I? and What am I? It is because we, ourselves, are not deeply rooted in the answers to those two questions that we waiver in the breezes of adversity and opposition. Therefore, we must find the answers to what we truly believe in The Church of Jesus Christ of Latter—Day Saints and gain such a solid testimony of them that we will never waiver again. Once we gain that confirmation for ourselves via our own powers of reasoning, we can and must turn to the Holy Ghost for solidifying the answers in our minds forever more.

Chapter 1   37

We are indebted to Elder Rex Pinegar (former President of the North America South East Area) for the following schematic illustration. It really helps us to understand the importance of these two questions in our lives. In fact, if we have not securely locked in on the answer to the question "Who am I?" by the age of five and to the answer to the question of "What am I?" by the age of eight, we are floundering. We must, therefore, go back and start over on these two questions as many times as necessary until all doubt has been burned out of our hearts and we are so totally convinced of the answers that we will never entertain even the shadow of a doubt ever again.

Those who are unlearned would define this approach to learning as indoctrination or brainwashing or blind obedience. They are surely entitled to their opinions. Yet, there are as many answers to these questions as there are religions, ways of life, or human philosophies, and many of them emerge from the same scripture with such differing thoughts. Can any of them be right and yet be so different?

An answer is not proposed or given to you here. You are to seek your own. What is suggested herein is an excellent and proven procedure so that you might find out the correct answer for yourself. Therefore, any suggestion of brainwashing, etc., is simply ludicrous.

To help you understand the illustration several basic points need to be made. For example, if we do not *know* that we are truly children of the living Father in Heaven by age five, our minds become filled with fear, doubt, and insecurity. If, on the other hand, we really do *know* this divine truth, we become so convinced of our identity, security, and love that we will never question it nor allow any one to invade our personal privacy to question it.

After controlling our thought processes, we can then construct the balance of our lives on the "rock" of the Savior rather than on the "sands" of men and Satan. In this Gender

Phase, to *know* is to begin to understand that "I am a child of God" is not merely as statement of nice sounding words, but the beginning of a "rock—like feeling experience" through which real knowledge develops to solidify in your mind that you truly are a child of God.

But many will say that a child of five could not possibly possess such a definitive knowledge of a sacred truth. Those who would feel this way do not understand that there is a Divine spark of trust that exists in two ways in a child of God. One is that every person born into this world has received the Light of Christ through which to obtain answers to eternal truths and one's age has nothing to do with Divine manifestations of the Spirit.

LIFE—LONG PERSONAL GROWTH SCHEMATIC

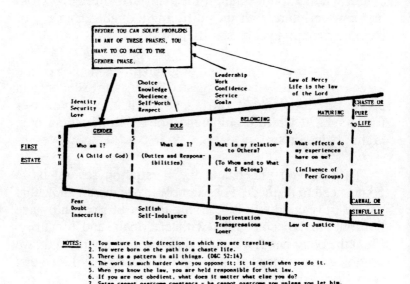

Chapter 1   39

The second is that in families, which develop a full flow of the everlasting Gospel in their homes, and who speak open and honestly about its teachings, provide a solid basis on which children place their testimonies until these are strong enough to stand alone. This is the true meaning of the Prophet Joseph Smith's injunction to "teach them correct principles and they will never depart therefrom."

Further, *"And that from a child thou hast known the holy scriptures, which are able to make thee wise unto salvation through faith which is in Christ Jesus"* (see 2 Timothy 3:15). To add to that interesting teaching, *"Train up a child in the way he should go: and when he is old [er], he will not depart from it"* (see Proverbs 22:6). And, while we are thus being instructed, *"...and a little child shall lead them"* (see Isaiah ll:6; 2 Nephi 21:6; 2 Nephi 30:12). Some of the most profound lessons we learn in life come from and through little children.

By the same concept, we must *know*, by the time we reach the age of eight, the answer to the question of "What am I?" Once we truly *know* that answer, we are in a strong position to exercise our freedom of choice in order to gain additional gospel knowledge, to develop our sense of internal self—worth, and to have a deep respect for sacred things, including our own minds and bodies. *"Once a person has a truer sense of his or her identity, the person is free to make more fulfilling choices"* (see Reader's Digest, *ABC's of the Human Mind*, p.33). To *know* what you are in this Role Phase is to have firmly planted in your mind the truth that you really are important to the Godhead as outlined in Abraham 3:23 and Alma 13:3.

If we never really come to know such an answer, our lives will be filled with selfishness and continued self—indulgence. The development of such negative values will result in our becoming anti—Christ in many ways because of weak testimonies, luke-warm service, and frequent withdrawal from Church activities for one reason or another. Included in such excuses will be finding fault with leaders and disagreement over revelations.

40   Where Art Thou

Obviously, we continue to grow in physical age despite our spiritual, emotional, or mental status regarding the answers to these two basic questions. By the age of sixteen, we must come to *know* the answer to yet a third basic question — "What is my relationship with others?"

This is the question that incorporates a feeling of "belonging". It develops the certainty within us as to whom and to what do we belong! The answers are derived from leadership experiences, our work ethic, and our desire to serve others within or without the Church. It is in the critical age period from eight to sixteen that these positive and important values develop, because it is in this Belonging Phase that we learn to rise above the mundane peer group influences and begin the implantation of deeper, higher feelings of interdependence with each individual member of the Godhead.

As these values develop, we learn how to set goals as well as what we must do to fulfil them. The success of such achievements establishes and increases our confidence to meet and overcome crises and real difficulties. Any failure on our part to develop our sense of belonging during this important eight—year period leaves us with a disorientation as to our true direction in life. It results in our frequent use of rationalizations to point the blame for our failures towards others and it puts a soothing ointment on our guilt so that we will not feel that we are at fault. Such a failure to "belong" is also the main reason why some individuals become "loners" who often feel that nobody really cares if they succeed or fail, so why even try.

Between ages sixteen to thirty, we endure the Maturing Phase in our lives. Slowly but surely, we begin to accept the fact that we cannot function successfully as individuals, that we do indeed need others to help us in various activities, and that all of our experiences have differing effects on our own perceptions and behaviors.

Chapter 1   41

It is in this age period that we must learn how to truly refine our interdependence with people as well as with the Godhead To do this, we must surrender our improper feelings of dependency and independency. Then, we must merge those which are proper into our most significant interdependency role of human emotions and behaviors. This we can do as we interact with those who are in our own personal theaters of operations, such as family, friends, work, or church, because we become increasingly aware that everything we do not only affects someone else, but also impacts upon our own lives.

Hopefully, it is during this age period that we realize the full realities of the Laws of Mercy and Justice. If we accept the fact that all that we have we owe to the Lord, we will then invoke the Law of Mercy upon ourselves by repenting fully. If we continue to act as loners, or if we persist in allowing peer group influences to control our lives, we will be unrepentant and the Law of Justice will demand full payment at some point in our second—estate existence.

Note the additional comments in the diagram previously given.

1. If you have problems in the belonging and/or maturing phases, you must return to the gender and/or role phases in order to solve them.

2. We mature in the direction in which we are traveling — Christ—like if we are chaste or Satan—like if we are carnal.

3. Since little children are born without sin, we automtically are placed by a loving God in the pathway for the living of a chaste life. If we fall to a carnal life, we do it on our own — without the Lord's help.

4. *" . . .I will give unto you a pattern in all things, that ye may not be deceived; for Satan is abroad in the land."* (see

D&C 52:14). You should remember that Gospel principles including your temple covenants and your patriarchal blessing are important parts of your personal pattern.

5. In the final analysis, we stand alone before the Savior to answer for our deeds: " . . .*every man may be accountable for his own sins in the day of judgment"* (see D&C 101:78).

If we refer back to the verses quoted from Job 4:3—6, we can review the truth that we can teach and help others rather easily. But when problems touch our own lives, we are troubled — sometimes deeply. We tend to lose our personal motivation as doubts flood our minds.

We can never totally eliminate such tendencies. We can, however, substantially reduce their effects if we follow the examples set by our Redeemer. Here are a few of them:

*The preparation of Jesus for His mission included both the pre—existence and mortality. We have already had our pre—existent preparation. Now we must capitalize on this mortal experience.

*Jesus was in total harmony with the Father. He was "anxiously engaged" with an eye single to the light. He demands no less from us and tells us that we must " . . .*be anxiously engaged in a good cause, and do many things of their own free will, and bring to pass much righteousness . . ."* (see D&C 58:26—28).

*We must care about others as much as we care about ourselves. Jesus denied Himself of all wrong feelings and He "lost" Himself in service to all who would come unto Him.

*The Savior constantly taught correct principles. He taught us what kind of people we ought to become - even as He. He wasted not His time on the philosophies of men mingled with scripture. He taught true Gospel principles.

Chapter 1   43

*No person has ever suffered as deeply as our Redeemer. He descended below all things in order to be in a position to pay the price of the sins of which we repent. He never wavered nor deviated. Why should we when any troubles visit us? In fact, even Jesus was stretched (remember the analogy of the rubber band) by having to carry His own cross, especially after He had already suffered great physical punishment at the hands of His tormentors.

*Jesus frequently gave thanks to His Heavenly Father for all of His blessings. Likewise, He commanded us that *"And ye must give thanks unto God in the Spirit for whatsoever blessing ye are blessed with"* (see D&C 46:32).

*Our Savior knew of His divine calling to be the Redeemer of all mankind. He knew and taught the principle of foreordination. Do you understand that Alma's reference in Chapter 13:3 to this same principle included you? *"And this is the manner after which they were ordained — being called and prepared from the foundation of the world according to the foreknowledge of God, on account of their exceeding faith and good works; in the first place being left to choose good or evil; therefore they having chosen good, and exercising exceedingly great faith, are called with a holy calling, yea, with that holy calling which was prepared with, and according to, a preparatory redemption for such."*

We were amongst those who were most faithful in the pre—existence, who were called, prepared, and ordained, who exercised exceeding faith and good works, and who have now been called to serve a holy calling. If you do not have a testimony of these truths, you must fast and pray and study in order to obtain it, for they are true.

Such a testimony will help you to cement your gender phase and your role phase as discussed earlier. It will be a strong factor in protecting you from motivational highs and lows in your devotion to our Heavenly Father. It will earn for you the accolade *"Peace, peace be unto you, because of your faith in my Well Beloved, who was from the foundation of the world"* (see Helaman 5:47).

Chapter Five

A TIME APPOINTED FOR EVERY MAN

D&C 121:25 — "For there is a time appointed for every man, according as his works shall be."

There are many fatalistic thinkers in the world who write or teach that an individual's life span is predetermined. Therefore, it is in the cards that when a person's "number" comes up, there is nothing that can be done to change it. Unfortunately, this point of view often serves only to provide the owner of it with an excuse to do anything and everything he or she desires to do and, at the same time, feel good about it.

This attitude is an excellent example of how Lucifer need only to distort the actual truth just a little in order to destroy man's objectivity, and hence the work of the Lord.

Job asked the question, *"Is there not an appointed time to man upon the earth? . . ."* (see Job 7:1). To which the Lord replied that, *" . . .Thy days are known, and thy years shall not be numbered less; therefore, fear not what man can do, for God shall be with you forever and ever"* (see D&C 122:9). Also, *" . . .but it was appointed unto men that they must die; . . ."* (see Alma 12:27).

President Brigham Young taught: *"It is not the design of our Father that the earthly career of any should terminate until they have lived their days; and the reason that so few do live out their days is because of the force of sin in the world and the power of death over the human family. So live that when you wake up in the spirit—world you can truthfully say, 'I could not better my mortal soul, were I to live it over again'* " (see *Discourses of Brigham Young*, p. 370).

In view of these correct teachings, it would appear to be a wise course of action if we were to concentrate on the eternal quality of our lives and leave the quantity of days and years to a very loving and wise Father and Son. It is our responsibility to be concerned about that quality and we cannot pass it off to another living soul. This sought—for quality is often directly related to our own attitude. W. E. Ziege wrote, *"Nothing can stop the man with the right attitude from achieving his goal; nothing on earth can help the man with the wrong attitude."*

In order to substantially raise the quality of our lives — should we desire to do so — we must first understand much more about our own individuality and uniqueness. Such an understanding serves not only to give us greater personal control over our journey but also a much deeper appreciation of the gender and role phases of our development as outlined in the preceding chapter.

There are many theories concerning the individual and his growth and development. Each seems to have some value. It would seem prudent, however, to concentrate on those which coincide with the principles of the revealed Gospel of Jesus Christ. It would be rather unwise to pursue any philosophy simply because it sounds or feels good. Those given in this chapter are those which can be defended by scripture and the writings of the Prophets.

Within each individual there is planted the seed of dignity which ensures us that we are capable of making our own decisions. This is why the Church leaders have ever empha- sized the criticality of teaching children correct principles

Chapter 1   47

when they are growing through the first eight years so that they will never depart far from them thereafter. If they do stray, those correct principles will be a source of irritation in their minds until repentance is effected. That is how the seed of dignity works.

Such a seed is also needed for us to sort out our eternal ideals when these conflict with our selfish desires. Our ideal is what we want to become — a long range objective. Our conscience, on the other hand, is not bashful in telling us what we actually are and what we think. When there is a discrepancy between our eternal ideals and desires and our conscience, the result is guilt, depression, lack of confidence, frustration, and frequent discouragement.

Elder H. Burke Peterson stated: *"We become what we think; we think about the things we hear, read, and see."* Elder Ezra Taft Benson taught that *"it is always good strategy to stand up for the right, especially when it is unpopular."* To continue the development of this seed of God—like dignity and to avoid destructive conflicts with our conscience, we must be wholly integrated into Christ's teachings. This promotes congruence between our self and our experience. Such congruence brings peace, direction, and eternal life. Congruence is to be the same as or identical to some object, ideal, or value.

As a child of God, created in His image, man is born basically good and trustworthy, but God has given us an advantage in the Spirit or Light of Christ. It is when we fail to listen to the Light that we get into trouble. For members of the Church the same concept applies to the Holy Ghost.

This occurs because much of our behavior is based on our perceptions which can be both right and wrong. More will be written on this very important understanding in Chapter Ten. Therefore, further development of this concept can await until then.

Each of us possesses an internal natural capacity for growing and developing. This capacity is often referred to as the "actualizing tendency." It incorporates an inherent inclination to develop all of our capabilities in those specific ways which serve to maintain or enhance our own individual ego, pride, and arrogance.

It is this actualizing tendency that becomes the primary motivational force for all of our actions including the active process in our minds which effects changes when such are necessary or inevitable. The reason that this motivating force has such strength is because we exist in a continually changing world of experiences in which we are the very center.

Because we are that center, we have the best vantage point from which to understand our own behavior. And most of the ways in which we behave are those which are consistent with our concept of self — right or wrong.

God has created us so that we are or can be much wiser than our own intellect. We do possess greater wisdom than our actions often imply. We frequently do "know better." If we can learn to function without always being defensive, we can develop a trust in our total behavior pattern. Thus, when faced with difficulties, that trust serves to sharpen, not dull, our awareness of our strengths and true capacities to survive and grow.

Our wise Father in Heaven did not grant unto us the power to control others. Yet we waste endless energies worrying about that and trying to change others amongst our circle of friends.

We can *influence* others. But, we only have the ability to be in *control* of ourselves. If we separate those things over which we have control from those over which we have no control, we could save ourselves many worries and much wasted energy. When we assume full control over our own lives, we can be proactive in developing those lives. Then, we can become truly interdependent with others, and our ability to be of help increases.

People fall into three categories — those who are depen-

Chapter 1   49

dent on others, those who want to live independently of others, and those who incorporate the desire to be interdependent with others. Hopefully, this latter includes the three members of the Godhead as we live our lives. (See *The 7 Habits of Highly Effective People*, by Stephen R. Covey)

Dependent people want others to take care of them and more often than not refuse to accept the blame for what they do. Good examples of dependent people are Laman and Lemuel who were always angry and discontent over lost leadership and the "lack of vision" by their father. Dependent people live in a very selfish **"ME"** centered world which they have created for their own purposes and which they frequently maintain by manipulating people — a skill often developed to a very high degree.

Independent people adopt the attitude that they do not need anyone else. They stress the fact that they have their free agency and can do whatever they have the urge to do whenever they want to do it. Their existence is an **"I"** centered one which is as selfish as the dependent mode of behavior. It represents a very false understanding of the principle of free agency as taught and practiced by the Savior. He demonstrated that free agency is always accompanied by responsibility. You can certainly choose the action but you can never select the reward or punishment that is assigned by the Lord to that action.

Obviously, the ideal category of people is the interdependent type. Alma informed us that " . . .*every thing shall be restored to its perfect frame, as it is now, or in the body, and shall be brought and be arraigned before the bar of Christ the Son, and God the Father, and the Holy Spirit, which is one Eternal God, to be judged according to their works, whether they be good or whether they be evil"* (see Alma 11:44). Inasmuch as we are going to be judged by the Godhead, it would seem a wise concept to incorporate each member thereof into our lives on a continuing basis.

In this respect, notice that the entry covenant into the

50   Where Art Thou

Gospel [baptism] is performed in the name of the Holy Trinity.
Add to this the fact that the crowning ordinance of the
Priesthood — temple marriage — is likewise performed. This
suggests the need for the Godhead. The best example of such
interdependency is the Savior Himself. His total unity with the
Father is beyond dispute. It was because of this that He was
able to provide for our eventual return to that same Father. His
interdependency incorporated the best features of dependency and independency because each of these were placed in
the proper perspective and role: that is, it demonstrated the
elimination of all unselfishness.

    Such a high quality of interdependency values differences
in other people, looks for the good in others, adds to your
repertoire of positive or negative experiences, increases greatly
your knowledge, and proves your integrity, which is the value
you place on yourself and on your ability to make and keep
commitments. This level of interdependency also adds personal
discipline to your principles and values as well as develops a
feeling of success from within your own self. Such growth is
priceless. It can be gained in no other way.

    The type of interdependency we are talking about is a
"WE" centered one. It represents the highest form of human
behavior that we are capable of developing and attaining. It is
Christ—like behavior at its finest. It brings the type of peace
spoken of by Jesus when He said *"Peace be unto thee."* It is
the peace that comes from feeling the Savior's loving arms
about you in times of need and blessing. Would you not want
to experience those loving arms embracing you? You can, but
it requires interdependency with the Father, the Son, and the
Holy Ghost over an extended period of time.

    Interdependency and proactivity go together. They are
driven by man's ability to control his own life. During his
terrible and torturous experience in a German concentration
camp, Victor Frankl discovered this very real, yet startling
concept. He came to understand fully that even though his

Chapter 1

liberty had been totally taken away from him, his tormentors could never remove from him his freedom of thought. Frankl had lost loved ones to the cruelties of the Gestapo and he had suffered all types of inhumane personal torture himself.

As a result of his discovery, he concluded that he could become the creator of his own life. When he realized that, he also awakened to the fact that man was not like Pavlov's dogs because man is capable of selecting one response from several available ones when he is subjected to a given stimulus. It was Frankl's observation that man, unlike animals, almost always has more than one alternative from which to choose when he is presented with a given stimulus. This makes much sense for man represents God's greatest creation.

Therefore, he must have the ability to always choose his responses or he would be little better than Pavlov's dogs. When he chooses his reactions, he is in control of his life. When this control interacts with others using God—given principles, he is functioning on a very high interdependent level.

Man had now discovered the truth taught by King Benjamin over two thousand years ago when he spoke *"But this much I can tell you, that if ye do not watch yourselves, and your thoughts, and your words, and your deeds, and observe the commandments of God, and continue in the faith of what ye have heard concerning the coming of our Lord, even unto the end of your lives, ye must perish, and now, O man, remember, and perish not"* (see Mosiah 4:30).

You see, God has given to each of us one ultimate goal, yet He has made each of us differently. He has given us only one Plan of Salvation. We all make the same covenants in the temple and in the Gospel. Yet our lives are quite dissimiliar. We live in different periods of time, countries, and families. Even within the same family, children are not the same. Could we be any more different than we already are? It is because of these dissimilarities that we can become truly interdependent

52   Where Art Thou

and proactive, and we are expected to develop and value these differences. No one, least of all the Savior, is trying to mold everyone into the same pattern.

However, we have to come together in a singleness of purpose in Christ. We must be unified and strengthened in His mission and His atonement. Paul understood this when he wrote about being strong in the faith: *"For the which cause I also suffer these things: nevertheless I am not ashamed: for I know whom I have believed, and am persuaded that he is able to keep that which I have committed unto him against that day"* (see 2 Timothy 1:12). Further, there is an old proverb from India that states: *"**What** we believe divides us; **Whom** we believe unites us."*

We are encouraged to use our free agency wisely, but we must come together in Christ. We must be unified and strengthened in His mission. There is no other way for us to come to the Father without coming to Christ first. We do not have to be the same in body, mind, and spirit. There is ample room for individuality and differences in the Gospel.

Our unity in the work must, however, reach the same level as Jesus Christ has with the Father. Otherwise, we could be likened unto the son who told the master that he would go but went not; or we would be like the barren fig tree with leaves but no fruit. By being completely responsible for our own actions, we assume a full partnership with the Father and the Son and the Holy Ghost. That is how we assume full control of our destiny, improve the quality of our lives, retain our individual differences, and live out our appointed days.

Chapter Six

GOD SHALL GIVE YOU KNOWLEDGE

D&C121:26 — "God shall give unto you knowledge by his Holy Spirit, yea, by the unspeakable gift of the Holy Ghost, that has not been revealed since the world was until now."

In one of the most meaningful scriptures, Nephi wrote, *"For behold, thus saith the Lord God: I will give unto the children of men line upon line, precept upon precept, here a little and there a little; and blessed are those who hearken unto my precepts, and lend an ear unto my counsel, for they shall learn wisdom; for unto him that receiveth I will give more; and from them that shall say, We have enough, from them shall be taken away even that which they have"* (see 2 Nephi 28:30).

This beautiful philosophy is the learning plan of God. It is His way for us to gain knowledge. However, we must not assume that the use of the verb "give" means a free gift. If you will re—read, then ponder, this scripture, a few solid principles begin to emerge.

*You learn at the rate which you adopt for yourself — no faster, no slower. Nephi said not a word about intelligence or age or training. The Lord will most certainly reveal personally to you line upon line and precept upon precept. It will be given to you through personal revelation but only as you make the

54   Where Art Thou

effort to learn and apply His truths. Knowledge will not be
granted free from effort. However, a person can acquire
education or information at any age, but he or she can only
obtain wisdom from the experiences obtained in applying that
knowledge and information.

***If you hearken unto the Lord's teachings, you will
obediently apply them in your life.** Then, you shall learn
wisdom which is the wise use of knowledge. To have wisdom
is far better than to have strength (see Ecclesiastes 9:16). The
Lord applies a punishment for disobedience. We know that.
But He also applies an equally severe penalty on those who
have had the opportunity to receive His commandments, but
who refuse to do so.

***Having carried out your responsibility for the above
two suggestions, the Lord promises you that He will give
you more.** So, a never—ending cycle is set into operation
which will not stop until you have gained a perfect knowledge
of all things. The Lord is prepared to deal with each of us on
this basis and He permits us to set the pace. However, we must
not delay our knowledge gains unnecessarily. A pace that is
too slow can be almost as disastrous as no pace at all.

***Those who give up, who feel that they have learned
enough, who refuse to do their part, or who turn away by
virtue of disobedience will forfeit much of what they have
already learned.** In the work of the Lord, no one can stand
still. We either are moving forward or we are slipping
backwards. Those who do the latter by virtue of disobedience
lose the opportunity for future learning of God's truths until
proper and true repentance takes place. You can never pick up
where you left off after you have transgressed the law.
Time has to be taken to repent properly. In using that
time, it results in a lost opportunity to continue learning. You cannot stand still; you have slipped backwards.
Therefore, you have to regain that which you could
have learned had it not been for the transgression.

Chapter 1   55

*The bottom line is that those who study, apply, and continually practice the truths of the Gospel not only come to *know* them but are also fortified in the use of them in every situation encountered along the path of life. Their progress will be steadily and firmly upward as they reach out to Christ. One, however, cannot live in the past nor in the future, only in the present moment. We learn from the past, and we plan for the future as we live each day.

The Lord instructed us as follows: *"Wherefore, honest men and wise men should be sought for diligently, and good men and wise men ye should observe to uphold; otherwise whatsoever is less than these cometh of evil. And I give unto you a commandment, that ye shall forsake all evil and cleave unto all good, that ye shall live by every word which proceedeth forth out of the mouth of God. For he will give unto the faithful line upon line, precept upon precept; and I will try you and prove you herewith"* (see D&C 98:10—12).

How does every word proceed forth out of the mouth of God? The answer is by revelation which comes to us in several ways. It can be our privilege to experience any or all of these ways.

At the top of the list, of course, is to actually see God and/ or Jesus Christ as did Joseph Smith, Stephen, or the Nephites. Next comes visitations from the Savior's messengers such as Moroni, Peter, James, John, Moses, Elias, Elijah, or John the Baptist. Other messengers may be ministering angels whose office *"...is to call men unto repentance, and to fulfil and to do the work of the covenants of the Father, which he hath made unto the children of men, to prepare the way among the children of men, by declaring the word of Christ unto the chosen vessels of the Lord, that they may bear testimony of him"* (see Moroni 7:31).

Other methods used to reveal the Lord's will to us include auditory and visual visions; direct or symbolic dreams; inspiration in such forms as feelings of peace, calm assurances,

56   Where Art Thou

positive or negative premonitions, answers from the scriptures, burnings of the bosom, stupors of thought, and a sense of being impelled to do or say something. In addition, the Light of Christ is still available to every male and female in the world and the Holy Ghost is a gift as a constant companion to every baptized member of the Church who lives worthily. The basic premise is that it is God who always determines the who, what, when, and where of revelation.

This basic premise is fundamentally true because we in our exhuberant ignorance would expect to use these avenues of revelation even when we are unworthy. In Romans, Chapters 6—8, Paul discusses the concept that when we learn truth, we also learn sin. He states: *"For they that are after the flesh do mind the things of the Spirit. For to be carnally minded is death; but to be spiritually minded is life and peace. Because the carnal mind is enmity against God: for it is not subject to the law of God, neither indeed can be"* (see Romans 8:5—7). When we are carnally minded, we close our minds to revelation and open them to sin.

With so many ways by which our Lord can give us constant guidance, what is there that prevents such blessed communication, other than enmity against God? It all comes down to the very basic question of what price are we willing to pay.

We are like the hourglass. All of our passions, desires, and values are in the top half. The narrow neck represents the degree to which we are willing to consecrate all that we have and are to the Lord. Some refuse to pay any price and the neck remains totally constricted [enmity against God].

Others want to pay a partial price. Hence, some grains of goodness dribble through the neck but not all. It is not until we are totally and completely centered on Jesus Christ that we become fully consecrated to His service. It is this degree of obedience, love, and service that permits all of our passions, desires, and values to move through the narrow neck to the bottom of the hour glass.

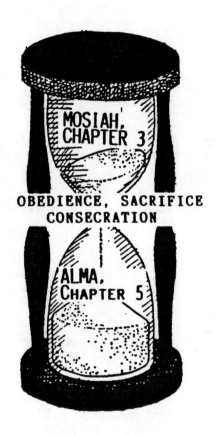

The upper part of this time piece is personified in Mosiah, Chapter 3 while the bottom portion is represented in Alma, Chapter 5. Draw your own conclusions from your careful and personal comparison. The following is offered as a starting point

Where Art Thou

Mosiah Chapter 3	Alma, Chapter 5
*Rebelleth against God (verse 12)	*Souls illuminated by the light of the everlasting word (verse 7)
*Stiffnecked with pride (verse 14)	*Bands of death broken (verse 8)
*Hardened hearts against teachings of the prophets, signs, and wonders (verse 15)	*Believed the words of the prophets (verse 11)
*Lack of humility (verse 18)	*Mighty change wrought in hearts (verse 12)
*Does not yield to the enticings of the Holy Spirit (verse 19)	*Humbled themselves (verse 13)
*Not submissive, meek, humble, patient, full of love, or willing to submit in all things to the Lord (verse 19)	*Put trust in true and living God (verse 13)
*Not blameless before God (verse 21)	*Faithful to the end (verse 13)
*Have a view of own guilt and abominations (verse 23)	*Spiritually born of God (verse 14)
*Shrink from the presence of the Lord (verse 23)	*Has His image in countenances (verse 14)
	*Look forward with an eye of faith (verse 15)
	*Works are works of righteousness (verse 17)
	*Look to God with a pure heart and clean hands (verse 19)
	*Sing the song of redeeming love (verse 26)
	*Righteous names are written in the book of life (verse 58)

It is quite obvious that the natural man could never be exalted. To transform from the natural man to the spiritual man requires time, effort, and devotion. It also demands that we study and learn according to God's plan for learning for we will constantly need His help if we are to earn His reward. It all begins with how badly you want to pay the price. Don't give up. God needs you and you need God.

Please review again the analogy of the hourglass as well as the comparative list of the teachings in Mosiah, Chapter 3 and Alma, Chapter 5. If you look carefully, you will see two threads of golden truth interwoven within them. One

Chapter 1

of threads is the principle of the Law of Sacrifice, and the second thread is the principle of the Law of Consecration.

Sacrifice means that we cannot develop an eternal character if we do not move through the narrow neck of the hourglass which represents the price we are willing to pay for our blessings. In moving through it for this Gospel principle, we are willing to sacrifice our appetites, passions, and human weaknesses. If we do this successfully, we will have the blessings of character and spirituality.

Of course, you can go through the mechanics of the law, but when the price becomes higher than you want to pay, or when the going gets rougher than you want to endure, you will back away. We absolutely cannot develop into exalted beings without obeying the Law of Sacrifice. The Lord surely understands those who go through the motions or who pay more attention to the letter of the law. The Pharisees and Sadducees provide the best example. *"They profess that they know God; but in works they deny him . . . "* (see Titus 1:16).

It is easy enough to be virtuous,
When nothing tempts you to stray,
When without or within no voice of sin,
Is luring your soul away;
But it's only a negative virtue,
Until it is tried by fire,
And the life that is worth the honor on earth,
Is the one that resists desire.

By the cynic, the sad, the fallen,
Who had no strength for the strife,
The world's highway is cumbered today,
They make up the sum of life;
But the virtue that conquers passion,
And the sorrow that hides a smile,
It is these that are worth the homage on earth,
For we find them but once in a while.
(Author Unknown)

60   Where Art Thou

The Law of Consecration is a celestial law, too. It is
inextricably intertwined with the development of the attributes of godliness in this life and the attainment of eternal
life in the world to come. When we are asked to live this law
in its fulness, we will have to root out every human trait that
is not in harmony with the requirements for living in the
Celestial Kingdom. It is worthy of note that a person who has
problems in living a lesser law, such as tithing and fast
offerings, will not be able to live the much higher law for
which the requirement is to give all.

If you use God's plan for learning, and if you are willing
to pay the full price of consecration, then you will be in the
same position as Nephi when he was addressed personally by
the Lord. *"Blessed art thou, Nephi, for those things
which thou hast done; for I have beheld how thou hast
with unwearyingness declared the word, **which I have
given unto thee**, unto this people. And thou hast not
feared them, and hast not sought thine own life, **but hast
sought my will**, and to **keep my commandments**. And
now, because thou hast done this with such
unwearyingness, behold, **I will bless thee forever**; and
I will make thee **mighty in word and in deed, in faith
and in works**; yea, even that all things shall be done
unto thee according to thy work, **for thou shalt not ask
that which is contrary to my will"** (see Helaman 10:4-5).

Chapter Seven

NOTHING SHALL BE WITHHELD

D&C 121:28 — "A time to come in the which nothing shall be withheld, whether there be one God or many gods, they shall be manifest."

When Joseph Smith went into the grove of trees on his father's farm, his one desire was to ask God in faith which church was true. Little did he expect to receive a personal manifestation from God the Father and His Only Begotten Son, Jesus Christ, through the power of the Holy Ghost, nor did he expect to be told that the true church was not on the earth, and that it would be his sacred calling to re—establish it.

That great and marvelous vision, however, served to clearly enunciate to the whole world the fact that there are three separate and distinct members in the Holy Trinity each with different missions but all perfected in harmony of purpose. In addition, that wonderful experience was the first in a continuing series of manifestations and visitations which established, and still establishes, the Dispensation of the Fulness of Times — the last dispensation in which nothing shall be withheld from man if he is true and faithful.

Each dispensation established by the Lord received its own authority. He told those who were chosen and ordained how to administer the ordinances necessary for eternal life.

62   Where Art Thou

This is why the words to be used in the ordinances such as baptism and administration of the Sacrament differ in each dispensation.

Throughout the Doctrine and Covenants, the term *new and everlasting covenant* is used in connection with the name of this dispensation. Many members often define the term new and everlasting covenant to be eternal marriage. This is an incorrect definition.

President Joseph Fielding Smith defined the new and everlasting covenant to be *"the fulness of the gospel composed of all covenants, contracts, bonds, obligations, oaths, vows, performances, connections, associations, and expectations that are sealed upon members of the Church by the Holy Spirit of Promise (Holy Ghost)."* This must be done by the authority of the President of the Church who holds the keys of the Aaronic and Melchizedek Priesthoods.

Thus, the new and everlasting covenant is the fulness of the Gospel as it is now being restored in this dispensation. Baptism is a new and everlasting covenant as is temple marriage. In fact, all covenants that we, as members of the Church, make with God are part of the new and everlasting covenant as it has been revealed and as it will yet be revealed to the living Prophet of God on earth at that time. That is the reason it is called the Dispensation of the Fulness of Times.

This new covenant was prophesied by Jeremiah who stated that the Lord had promised to *"...make a new covenant with the house of Israel, and with the house of Judah,"*...*"*a covenant which would lead to that glorious millenial condition in which"...*"they shall teach no more every man his neighbor, and every man his brother saying, Know the Lord: for they shall all know me, from the least of them unto the greatest of them, saith the Lord..."* (see Jeremiah 31:31—34).

The Prophet Joseph Smith taught that *"we are the favored*

Chapter 1

people that God has made choice to bring about the Latter—day glory; it is left to us to see, participate in and help roll forward the Latter—day glory, the 'dispensation of the fulness of times', when God will gather together all things that are in heaven, and all things that are upon the earth even as one" (see *Teachings of the Prophet Joseph Smith*, pp. 231—232).

The Lord reinforced this when He said, *"Verily, I say unto you, blessed are you for receiving mine everlasting covenant, even the fulness of my gospel, sent forth unto the children of men, that they might have life and be made partakers of the glories which are to be revealed in the last days, as it was written by the prophets and apostles in days of old"* (see D&C 66:2).

There can be little doubt in any of our minds that this last dispensation will bring to light those things that have been revealed in all former dispensations as well as other truths that have not been revealed to the people of this earth. We frequently read in the Book of Mormon that the prophets were commanded not to write certain words. These, too, shall come forth. All of this is, and will be, for our salvation as well as to prepare the world for the glorious return of the Savior when He ushers in the Millenial Kingdom and restores the earth to its paradisiacal glory (terrestrial glory) preparatory for the completion of His divine mission *" . . .to bring to pass the immortality and eternal life of man"* (see Moses 1:39).

Having accepted the gospel in its fulness, we have agreed and covenanted that we will keep the commandments of God for these two purposes. As we draw nearer and nearer to the Second Coming of Jesus Christ, it is painfully obvious that Lucifer will unleash all of his forces of evil upon the minds of men and women and children everywhere. What does he have to lose by that intensified attack? Obviously, he has nothing to win either. He just seeks to make each and every one of us as miserable and as pathetic as he himself is.

It is equally obvious as to why the Lord saved many of His

64   Where Art Thou

choicest spirits to come forth in these the last days. He trusts,
loves, and depends upon you. This fact has already been
attested to in previous chapters. It is also contained in many of
the patriarchal blessings given to numerous members of the
Church in these times, particularly today's youth. That is why
such youth are referred to as the "royal generation." Yours is
the decision as to whether or not you will fulfill your glorious
destiny and heritage. No one else can or will make it for you.

Reference is often made to the fact that we are in a battle with
Satan. The time for the battle is past. We are in an all—out war.
Military commanders are trained to save a strong force in reserve
and to commit them at such a point in the battle when they will
ensure the destruction of the enemy and positively influence the
victory. **YOU ARE THE LORD'S RESERVE** and you have
been committed to the war, not just the battle or skirmish. Will
you be an influence in His victorious mission?

There will be numerous occasions when the only peace
available to you will be in your own heart and soul and mind
— but it will be the peace that comes because you are deeply
committed to and involved in the processes of justification
and sanctification as discussed in Chapters Two and Three.
You should also remember the fact that you must be a part of
this statement: *"These are they who are just men made perfect
through Jesus the mediator of the new covenant, who wrought
out this perfect atonement through the shedding of his own
blood"* (See D&C 76:69). You may not be perfect yet, but as
you walk that path the same blessings of love, peace, and
protection will be showered out upon you.

We are *"to have the privilege of receiving the mysteries of the
kingdom of heaven, to have the heavens opened unto them, to
commune with the general assembly and church of the Firstborn,
and to enjoy the communion and presence of God the Father, and
Jesus the mediator of the new covenant"* (see D&C 107:19).

Truly the heavens were opened to Joseph Smith in the

Chapter 1   65

Sacred Grove. The heavens continued to be open to him as well as to all other prophets of this dispensation for the receipt of revelation for the Church as a whole. They have also been opened to and for us individually as members of this Church in order to receive the love, guidance, and inspiration that we need as individuals, and as faithful covenant—makers in these the last days.

Frank Leahy, the great football coach at Notre Dame University for many years, often used this motivational theme, *"When the going gets tough, the tough get going."* The "going" in this dispensation will get much tougher. Of that, there can be absolutely no doubt. Unfortunately, when our lives do experience rough spots, many individuals waiver and doubt and fall as they lose the faith. Maltie D. Babcock stated: *"The tests of life are to make, not break us."* What will they be for you? The present Notre Dame football coach teaches the pain is temporary but victory is forever.

Norman Vincent Peale offers us some stimulating thoughts in his book *You Can If You Think You Can*. It is suggested that you place these thoughts in your spiritual bucket, as shown on Page 57 . Draw on them as well as on the scriptures whenever the going even begins to get tough. Do not wait for the trial to even develop if you can help it. Nip it in the bud by drawing on your spiritual bucket. You must, however, keep adding to your spiritual bucket. Deposits are so necessary in any account before you can make withdrawals.

*Believe that you have inherent in your mind all the resources you need to overcome many of your problems. There are many great concepts and helps stored in your mind awaiting only the correct stimulus for instant recall.

*Build up your resources by faith, learning, and know—how. Learning has to be ongoing. Brigham Young constantly encouraged everyone to look for truth in all subjects. The Lord said, *"And as all have not faith, seek ye diligently and teach one another words of wisdom; yea, seek ye out of the best* *books words of wisdom; seek learning, even by study and also by faith"* (see D&C 88:ll8).

*Remember that spiritual power activates your forces of mind and spirit. It serves as a motivation. Psychologist William James said: *"The greatest discovery of my generation is that human beings can alter their lives by altering their attitudes of mind."* Develop a hunger for spiritual power and your behavior will follow suit.

*Such motivation reveals all of your own talents and potential. People who live in the past usually lack motivation. Charles F. Kettering, the great inventive genius, once remarked, *"I am not interested in the past. I am interested only in the future, for that is where I expect to spend the rest of my life."* Family history researchers are often accused of living in the past. In reality, they may be amongst the most forward looking group of people because all they do is for the future blessing of their kindred dead.

*Don't be a hold—out or a half—a—minder: be an all—out. Implement your creative ideas with your whole mind — that is, both the right and left halves of your brain. Go all out and make things happen. This is what is meant by being proactive. William James stated: *"There is no more miserable human being than one in whom nothing is habitual but indecision."* There is a deep thrill that comes to people who reach into the inner center of their minds and pull out upper level emotional, spiritual, physical, or intellectual responses to difficult and seemingly impossible problems and challenges.

*Never minimize your ability to think your way through any situation. Remember the example of the brother of Jared. He asked the Lord to provide light for the barges. He wanted the Lord to solve his problem for him. The Lord virtually told him to solve his own problem (see Ether 2:23). This he did with the sixteen stones. As a result, he was blessed to see the Savior — first His finger and then His entire spirit body. He

Chapter 1   67

was told also that because of his faith, he " . . .*was brought back into my presence . . .*" (see Ether 3:13). Too many individuals find it easier to "ask someone else." In doing this, there is no growth. The Lord has told us to work out the solution to our problem in our mind first, then ask Him and if it be right, we will have a burning in our bosom. If it be wrong, we will have a stupor of thought (see D&C 9:7—9).

*Be bold, and mighty powers will come to your aid. Too many of us fear man more than we do God. Perhaps that is because the "man" in our lives is here and now, whereas God is "out there." Nevertheless, it is not the "man" who helps us when judgment time comes. To think that way is to have tunnel vision. Fear frequently causes us to adopt a policy of appeasement which ultimately pleases no one and destroys everyone. Alma taught his son Shiblon, *"Use boldness, but not overbearance; and also see that ye bridle all your passions, that ye may be filled with love; see that ye refrain from idleness"* (see Alma 38:12). Funnel vision is what we must use in developing our powers. We must continually strive to see the "big" picture.

*Never bog down in a defeatist psychology — keep looking for victory. If you carry around in your mind from one day to the next a load of dejection because things haven't gone as well as you had hoped or planned, you will soon run completely out of energy. Henry Thoreau taught that men are born to succeed, and Ralph Waldo Emerson declared: *"Self—trust is the first secret of success."* You cannot possibly carry the whole world on your shoulders nor were you ever intended to do that. Remember, you can only eat an elephant in small bites.

*In adversity, keep motivated for often the best comes from difficulty. William A. Ward stated: *"Adversity causes some men to break; others to break records."* Many successful business people, such as J. C. Penney, credit adversity as the secret for their successes because it made them work harder and appreciate their achievements more. Another example is Colonel Harland Sanders, who was a failure at

68   Where Art Thou

sixty—five, became world famous and a proudly acclaimed business success at eighty as the Kentucky Fried Chicken King.

*Imagine your goal — always keep it before you and it will eventually materialize. Many Christians think that all roads lead to heaven. We know that this is a false concept. Nevertheless, it would appear that many members of the Church have no clear—cut road map for their journey towards Exaltation. They seem to be content to just let it happen. For example, look at how few study the lessons ahead of time or even bother to carry their scriptures to Church with them. It is a good policy to live one day at a time, but that day must be a part of a definitive course of action plan that is clearly set in your mind. If you do not know exactly where you are going and what you must do each day to get there, you will never know when you have arrived, or even if you have reached the correct destination.

So much knowledge is pouring forth in this last dispensation. Do not be overwhelmed. Use the Lord's plan for learning as already discussed. Keep reminding yourself that you are a child of God who is often greater than you think you are. You are better than you give yourself credit for being.

By developing and capitalizing on your Divine parentage and by being obedient to all of the commandments of this new and everlasting Gospel, you, like Joseph Smith, can see the Savior. *"For they will hear my voice, and shall see me, and shall not be asleep, and shall abide the day of my coming; for they shall be purified, even as I am pure"* (see D&C 35:21).

There is a theoretical club in the world entitled "The—old—too—soon, wise—too—late—club." Don't become a member of it, not even accidentally. Do your part to learn all that you can as fast as you can. The Lord will surely do His part in helping you by opening up the windows of heaven and pouring out understanding and comprehension upon you. Thus, your knowledge will continually be increasing and you will interact with each member of the Holy Trinity as you were

Chapter 1   69

ordained and set apart to do from before the foundations of the earth.

The scripture used at the beginning of this chapter stated that we are living in a time when nothing will be withheld from us, including a knowledge of the Godhead. So far, we have concerned ourselves with how we learn and how we can better understand and develop ourselves so that we can learn in a superior way.

The reason we have spent so much time on this phase of that scripture is that very few of us will ever have a personal visit from the Godhead as did Joseph Smith. At least, such an experience may not have happened to us already. We are expected to master ourselves and develop our own talents before we can rightfully expect the "extraordinary" from God.

It is now important that we look at the reference to the Godhead as given in D&C 121:28, because there are very few human beings in the world who correctly understand the character of God. If His character is misunderstood, so will be His form, power, priesthood, and purpose. Further, if people do not understand the character of God, they will not comprehend themselves because they are created in the image of God.

Joseph Smith stated: *"God himself was once as we are now, and is an exalted man, and sits enthroned in yonder heavens. That is the great secret. If the veil were rent today, and the great God who holds this world in its orbit, and who upholds all worlds and all things by his power, was to make himself visible — I say, if you were to see him today, you would see him like a man in form — like yourselves in all the person, image, and very form as a man; for Adam was created in the very fashion, image, and likeness of God, and received instruction from, and walked, talked and conversed with him, as one man talks and communes with another"* (see Teachings of the Prophet Joseph Smith, p. 345).

Joseph Smith offered us his own personal testimony for he saw the Father and the Son in the Sacred Grove. Yet when he

70   Where Art Thou

went forth to various ministers, they laughed at and reviled him. Even today, there are literally millions of people who cannot and will not accept the fact that as man now is, God once was, and as God now is, man may become. To such people, this teaching is heresy, completely unbelievable, and totally unacceptable — and this from the minority who even accept Him as their Savior. There are still millions and millions who will not follow Christ in any form.

It is the unequivocal doctrine of the Church that there are two personages who constitute the great governing and supreme power of all things, by whom all things were created and made. They are the Father and the Son.

The Father possesses all perfection and fulness as well as glory and power. He is a personage of all knowledge. He is literally the Father of our spirits. In comparison, the Son was made in the Father's express image and likeness as were we all. He is called the Son because of the flesh and because Elohim was the literal father of His Son.

Jesus Christ descended in suffering below all that man can suffer or sin. Thus, He endured greater sufferings and was exposed to more powerful contradictions than any man could ever be. He kept the law of God and remained without sin. He was the Jehovah of the Old Testament, the Jesus Christ of the New Testament, and the Restorer of this dispensation. Because he gave all, redeemed all, and loves all, the way has been opened by Him for any one of us to return to our Heavenly Father.

These two supreme beings, when united with and operating through the Holy Ghost, comprise the Holy Trinity. The Holy Ghost bears record of the Father and the Son to all who will listen. The three members of the Godhead possess the same mind, wisdom, glory, power, and fulness because they are all united in purpose.

In one of the most powerful testimonies ever recorded, we

Chapter 1   71

read, *"And now, after the many testimonies which have been given of him, this is the testimony, last of all, which we give of him: That he lives! For we saw him, even on the right hand of God; and we heard the voice bearing record that he is the Only Begotten of the Father — that by him, and through him, and of him, the worlds are and were created, and the inhabitants thereof are begotten sons and daughters unto God"* (D&C 76:22—24).

Of all people who ever lived, we, as members of the only true church on the earth, should know the true character of God. God the Father and Jesus Christ the Son are not mysterious essences or intangible substances without form, body, parts, or passions; who fill the immensity of space while being small enough to dwell in the hearts of men. They are not part of a trinity that is one in substance but of unknown origin and destiny.

If any one of us lacks the sure knowledge and testimony of the Godhead we worship, let him pay the price to find out. The truth will never be withheld from one who sincerely fasts, studies, prays, and asks. When the search has been completed for each truth, the person will experience internal feelings of peace and testimony. Someone once said, *"I walked quiet paths in search of peace, but peace eluded me until I found it within."*

72 Where Art Thou

Chapter Eight

WHO HAVE ENDURED VALIANTLY

D&C 121:29 — "All thrones and dominions, principalities and powers, shall be revealed and set forth upon all who have endured valiantly for the gospel of Jesus Christ."

Do you ever, during times of quiet introspection, ponder the more solemn and sacred mysteries of life? Missionaries ask investigators three very basic yet critical questions such as "Where did we come from? Why are we here? and Where are we going?" For the purpose of this publication, you are asked to think profoundly about "What is our relationship to God the Father? and "What do we have to do to ensure eternal family relationships?"

The answers to these questions are not found in the wisdom of men. They are found only in the revealed word of God as contained in the scriptures and as taught in the House of the Lord, a place of instruction, of holiness, and of peace. The temple of the Lord is the university of God. In it, eternal and basic principles are taught during the performance of sacred ordinances which bring to our attention, and place in proper perspective, the knowledge of the truth. This is designed to motivate us to understand our divine inheritance as a child of God who can succeed in our most sacred commitments.

These ordinances are so valuable and sacred that they are

74   Where Art Thou

available only to those who qualify through righteous living. Once received, many blessings come to us if we honor, apply, and expand the knowledge and covenants that we learn in the temple of God. These are absolutely necessary for our exaltation.

We are told by Elder James E. Talmage that *"no jot, iota, or tittle of the temple rites is otherwise than uplifting and sanctifying. In every detail the endowment ceremony contributes to covenants of morality of life, consecration of person to high ideals, devotion to truth, patriotism to nation, and allegiance to God"* (see *The House of the Lord*, p. 84).

The designation of certain buildings for special ordinances is not new. This was the practice in ancient Israel, where the people worshipped regularly in the synagogues. Their more sacred place was, first, the tabernacle in the wilderness with its Holy of Holies, followed by a succession of temples, such as Solomon's, the rebuilding of his temple under the patronage of King Cyrus, and Herod's to which the Savior was taken when twelve years of age.

In these temples, special ordinances were performed. Only those who met the specific and required qualifications could participate in those ordinances. Then, as now, the work that goes on in our present temples sets forth God's eternal purposes for man — the child and creation of God. For the most part, it is concerned with the family — with each of us as a member of God's eternal family and with our own earthly family. It is concerned with the sanctity and eternal nature of the marriage covenant and with the resultant family relationships.

Temple work affirms that each man and woman born into the world is a child of God endowed with something of His divine nature. Thus, each is a member of His divine family. Hence, every man is your brother and every woman is your sister in that patriarchal family based on the highest order of the priesthood. This gives great emphasis to the need for love in that eternal family unit. In fact, it would be very, very difficult for any of us

Chapter 1   75

to be obedient to our temple covenants without a full implementation of a full measure of love in our lives.

When asked by the scribe, *"Which is the first commandment of all?"* the Savior replied, *"And thou shalt love the Lord thy God with all thy **heart**, and with all thy **soul**, and with all thy **mind**, and with all thy **strength**: this is the first commandment. And the second is like, namely this, Thou shalt love thy neighbor as thyself. There is none other commandment greater than these"* (see Mark 12:28,30—31). By this instruction, the Lord centered all eternal values in the principle of love. He was also teaching us that love is a process and not a destination. That process is the source of our motivation that we need to want to live in God's family forever.

The teachings set forth in modern temples give powerful emphasis to this most fundamental concept of man's duty to his Father, to his Master, and to his brother. Sacred ordinances amplify this ennobling philosophy of the family of God. They teach that the spirit within each of us is eternal, in contrast to the body which is mortal.

They not only give us an understanding of these great truths, but they also motivate us towards a deeper love of God. In addition, they encourage us to demonstrate a more righteous neighborliness towards others all of whom are our Father's children.

Accepting the premise that we are children of God gives us a divine purpose in mortal life. As the revealed truth is taught in the House of the Lord, we truly realize that we lived as spirit children with Him and that we were indeed created by Him. By accepting His teachings, we became worthy to come here. The scriptures bear testimony of our creation, *"Before I formed thee in the belly I knew thee; and before thou camest forth out of the womb I sanctified thee, and I ordained thee a prophet unto the nations"* (see Jeremiah 1:5).

76   Where Art Thou

We came into this life as children of mortal parents and as members of families. Parents are partners with God in bringing to pass His eternal purposes for His children. The family, therefore, is a divine institution — the most important one in both mortality and in eternity. In fact, the most treasured and satisfying as well as the most beautiful and meaningful of all human relationships in mortality are found in a "together forever" family. This is particularly true in an eternal family that works together in harmony and cohesiveness towards Exaltation in the Celestial Kingdom.

The Lord stated in very clear language, *"And again, verily I say unto you, if a man marry a wife by my word, which is my law, and by the new and everlasting covenant, and it is sealed unto them by the Holy Spirit of Promise, by him who is anointed, unto whom I have appointed this power and the keys of this priesthood; and it shall be said unto them — Ye shall come forth in the first resurrection; and shall inherit thrones, kingdoms, principalities, and powers, dominions, all heights and depths— "....." and they shall pass by the angels, and the gods, which are set there, to their exaltation and glory in all things, as hath been sealed upon their heads, which glory shall be a fulness and a continuation of the seeds forever and ever"* (see D&C 132:19).

Thus, Exaltation in the Celestial Kingdom is reserved for those who meet the highest honors of heaven by making and then keeping these very important covenants. The formal ordinance, which the Lord has appointed for us to signify to Him that we personally accept all of the terms and conditions of the eternal gospel covenant, is that of baptism.

When we enter the waters of baptism we are expressing our willingness to take upon ourselves the name of Jesus Christ. Thereafter, each Sunday, we renew that blessing and willingness by partaking of the Sacrament. In addition, as we eat the bread and drink the water, we are witnessing our willingness to participate in the sacred ordinances of the temple and to receive the highest blessings made available to

Chapter 1   77

us through the name of and by the authority of Jesus Christ when He chooses to confer them upon us and when we are ready to receive them.

In this context, baptism becomes the entry ordinance to all others. The Sacrament reminds us of His wounded body and shed blood. Then, after going to the temple and receiving the additional covenants of the Priesthood, including the crowning ordinance of marriage, the Sacrament becomes the reminder of all of the blessings and covenants so generously provided by our loving Savior. It is very critical that we recognize the fact that by partaking of the Sacrament we are covenanting that we will always remember Him, that we will keep His commandments, and that we will live by every word that proceedeth forth from the mouth of God.

One additional point needs to be made regarding baptism. It provides the key to each of us for entrance into the Celestial Kingdom and we cannot enter without it. The rest of the ordinances, including those of the temple, are for entrance into Exaltation in that kingdom. No person can be exalted without all of these ordinances being in place and being honored. We are not really interested in baptizing people into the Telestial or Terrestrial Kingdoms.

"The Temple Endowment comprises instruction relating to the significance and sequence of past dispensations, and the importance of the present as the greatest and grandest era in human history. This course of instruction includes a recital of the most prominent events of the creative period, the condition of our first parents in the Garden of Eden, their disobedience and subsequent expulsion from that blissful abode, their condition in the lone and dreary world when doomed to live by labor and sweat, the plan of redemption by which the great transgression may be atoned, the period of the great apostasy, the restoration of the Gospel with all its ancient powers and privileges, the absolute and indispensable condition of personal purity and devotion to the right in present life, and a

78   Where Art Thou

strict compliance with Gospel requirements."

"The ordinances of the endowment embody certain obli-gations on the part of the individual, such as a covenant and promise to observe the law of strict virtue and chastity, to be charitable, benevolent, tolerant, and pure; to devote both talent and material means to the spread of truth and the uplifting of the race; to maintain devotion to the cause of truth; and to seek in every way to contribute to the great preparation that the earth will be ready to receive her King — the Lord Jesus Christ. With the taking of each covenant and the assuming of each obligation a promised blessing is pronounced, contingent upon the faithful observance of the conditions" (see James E. Talmage, *The House of the Lord*, pp. 83—84).

The temple covenants enrich us in at least four ways as follows:

1. We are endowed with power from on high. Thus, we can overcome all trials and temptations if we are completely and truly obedient.

2. We are endowed with information and knowledge that is relative to the Lord's purposes and plans in the creation and peopling of this earth, and which is necessary for our exalta-tion. The correct application of this knowledge places us on the road to justification and sanctification.

3. We are prepared to be sealed at the temple altar which adds to our glorious blessings, honors, and powers. This is the crowning ordinance of the Priesthood. It is what President Ezra Taft Benson referred to as being married in the right place by the proper authority for the right reason. The right reason is simply but strongly enunciated in D&C 131:1—4: *"In the celestial glory there are three heavens or degrees; and in order to obtain the highest, a man must enter into this order of the priesthood [meaning the new and everlasting covenant of marriage]; and if he does not, he cannot obtain it. He may*

enter into the other, but that is the end of his kingdom; he cannot have an increase."

4. We place ourselves in a position to receive the sanctifying and cleansing power of the Holy Ghost, thus becoming clean and spotless before the Lord. In addition, the experiences that a person receives in the temple probably results in a much, much deeper appreciation and use of the Holy Ghost than any other single activity or blessing.

As stated earlier, the ordinances of the temple are so sacred that they are not open to the view of the public. Because we stress this sacredness so much, there is a tendency on the part of some Church members to distort the place, role, and importance of the covenants. One of the results of this distortion has been a tendency on the part of some young people to conclude that the covenants can and should be stored in some safe place so that they will not ever be lost or disobeyed. This results in a condition that this writer often refers to as "tunnel vision."

If we look at our covenants with tunnel vision, this is what we see:

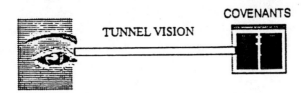

As you can determine, we will see only a very small portion of the covenants at any one time. In fact, we will generally see only what we want to see as we use our power to rationalize the type of behavior that suits us at the time and in which we will not really feel very bad. This ultimately will result in a psychological separation occurring in our minds between our daily activities and our obligations under the temple covenants; and the power of the latter will become less and less with the passage of time.

The desired alternative is to teach ourselves diligently to incorporate all of our covenants into every phase of our daily existence. This can only be achieved if we develop what the writer refers to as "funnel vision," a depiction that looks like this:

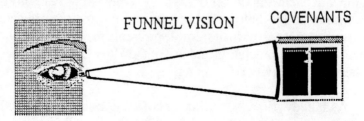

This allows us to keep in mind the "big picture" of the Lord's mission as well as our ultimate destiny. We will develop internally in our minds the psyche that our covenants and everyday living are totally and completely identical. One cannot and must not separate these or the result will be disastrous to our eternal lives. It is far better for us to use funnel vision because we will come to accept the fact that our covenants form the blueprint given by a loving Father in Heaven for our happiest living and most peaceful existence.

Elder Heber C. Kimball recorded in his journal the text of a talk given by Amasa Lyman in the Nauvoo Temple. The record reads: *"It is not for amusement you are brought to receive these things, but to put you in possession of the means of salvation, and be brought into a proper relationship to God. It is not designed that the things that are presented today should be forgotten tomorrow, but be remembered and practiced through all life."*

"Hence it is a stepstone to approach to the favor of God. Having descended to the lowest state of degradation, it is the beginning of a homeward journey: it is like a man lost in the wilderness, and the means with which we are invested here are to direct us in our homeward journey. No impression which you receive here should be lost."

"The scenery through which you have passed is actually laying before you a picture or map, by which you are to travel

Chapter 1   81

*through life, and obtain an entrance into the Celestial King-
dom hereafter. The principles which have been opened to you
are the things which ought to occupy your attention all your
lives. They are not second to anything; you have the key by
which, if you are faithful, you will claim on your posterity all
the blessings of the Priesthood"* (Helen M. Whitney, "Scenes
in Nauvoo and Incidences from Heber C. Kimball's Journal,"
1—15 August 1883, pp. 26,34).

The basic law upon which all of these obligations and
blessings rest is that of obedience. It is the first law of heaven and
therefore the foundation upon which the other covenants are
built. *" . . .the Lord is not bound, unless you keep the covenant.
The Lord never breaks his covenant. When he makes a covenant
with one of us, he will not break it. If it is going to be broken, we
will break it. But when it is broken, he is under no obligation to
give us the blessing, and we will not receive it . . ."* (see Joseph
Fielding Smith, *Doctrines of Salvation* 2:256—57).

The main roadblocks to our being fully obedient are lazy
apathy, lack of understanding, slothfulness, and fear of being
different in a Christ—like way. The Lord tells us that *"And Zion
cannot be built up unless it is by the principles of law of the
celestial kingdom . . ."* (see D&C 105:5). Therefore, we must
work continuously to set aside and overcome these negative
influences. These laws are too important to us to do less than
our very, very best for there is no satisfaction available for us
otherwise. These are eternal laws.

*"The law of sacrifice is a celestial law; so is the law of
consecration. Sacrifice and consecration are inseparably
connected. The law of consecration is that we consecrate our
time, our talents, and our energy to the work of the Church.
The law of sacrifice is that we are willing to sacrifice all that
we have for the sake of truth — our character, our reputation,
our honor, our applause, our families, even our very lives if
need be"* (Elder Bruce R. McConkie). Both of these laws
require complete obedience and an overcoming of the afore-

82   Where Art Thou

mentioned roadblocks.

Is it any wonder, then, why the gate is narrow and only a
few will find it? *"The great calamity, as I see it, is when you
or I with so much potential grow very little. That is the
calamity — when I could be so much and I am so little; when
I am satisfied with mediocrity in proselyting, in dentistry, in
teaching, in whatever I am going to do with my life; when I am
satisfied with this, oh, that is a sad, sad day because it has an
everlasting and eternal influence upon me. Why will only a few
reach exaltation in the celestial kingdom? Not because it was
not available to them, not because they did not know of its
availability, not because the testimony was not given to them,
but because they will not put forth the effort to pattern their
lives and make them like the Savior's life and establish {their
covenants} so well that there will be no deviation until the
end"* (see Spencer W. Kimball, *The Teachings of Spencer W.
Kimball,* pp. 173,51).

The endowment also offers to us the sanctifying and
cleansing power of the Holy Ghost so that we can become
clean and spotless before the Lord. The requirement is total
obedience to the covenants including complete consecration
of ourselves to the work in every calling to which we are called
to serve. The final step in our journey is the sealing ordinance
which seals us to Christ (Mosiah 5:15), seals us to our
companion (D&C 131:1—4), seals us to our parents (D&C
138:48), seals us in the patriarchal priesthood (Abraham 2:9—
11), and seals us into the Family of God (D&C 132:7—17).

In a previously quoted scripture (D&C 132:19), the Lord
promises those who are true and faithful to all of the temple
covenants certain specific blessings. These include, but are
not limited to, thrones, kingdoms, principalities, powers, and
dominions. The following explanations are offered.

Thrones — reserved for exalted persons who rule and
reign as kings and queens in the highest heaven of the celestial

Chapter 1   83

kingdom (see D&C 88:107). After Christ has presented up the kingdom to His Father, *"Then shall he be crowned with the crown of his glory, to sit on the throne of his power to reign forever and ever"* (see D&C 76:108). Then shall all those who are joint—heirs with Christ also sit upon their thrones and even sit down with our Lord on His throne.

Kingdoms — refers to the Celestial Kingdom which is the Kingdom of God and which does not include either the terrestrial or telestial kingdoms (see D&C 20:9; 2 Nephi 9:18,23). When a husband and wife become King and Queen, they have the power to create their own kingdoms as well as to have their own spirit children. In addition to these broader truths, the term "kingdom" can also be used as a shadow of good and heavenly things to come (see Hebrews 10:1; 8:5). We are such a shadow when we build and perpetuate solid, meaningful family traditions and customs.

Principalities — refers to the authorities by which all things are created (Colossians 1:16;2:10; 1 Peter 3:22). These are the governments or authorities used by a righteous King to direct the affairs of the families living under his supervision.

Powers — God has all power and there is no power he does not have. Those who obtain exaltation will gain all power and will thus be omnipotent (D&C 76:95; 88:107; 132:12—26). *"Then shall they be gods, because they have no end; therefore shall they be from ever-lasting to everlasting, because they continue; then shall they be above all, because all things are subject unto them. Then shall they be gods, because they have all power, and the angels are subject unto them"* (see D&C 132:20).

Dominions — mean to have special places reserved for us in which celestial mansions have been prepared (D&C 76:111). Those who attain exaltation will be equal in power, and in might, and in dominion to the Lord. These dominions are eternal ones and consist of the glory, authority, majesty, and

84   Where Art Thou

power which Jehovah possesses, and nothing less.

Hands — the couple to be married hold hands during
the ceremony. This act points the bride and groom to the
Savior and to His supreme sacrifice on the cross and in
the Garden of Gethsemane.

Receive — the groom is asked to receive the bride as his
wife. This has to be done by him without any qualifications,
reservations, or conditions. He is receiving a daughter of God
"as is," not **"as he wants her to be."** He is receiving a whole
person for the whole journey. As a full partner, he is responsible for surrounding his wife with a Christ—like atmosphere
so that he can help her become all that she can become in the
presence of the Father, and the Son, and the Holy Ghost.

Give — the bride is to give herself to the groom, but he is
under the same obligation to give himself to her. He is to give
to her the Holy Priesthood after the Order of the Son of God.
She is not giving or transferring ownership of herself to him.
She is entrusting him with her heart and with her sacred future
in his righteous exercise of the power of that Holy Priesthood.
If she is to enter Exaltation as his wife, he must take her and
that requires faithful use of the priesthood with all of its
attendant responsibilities.

Multiply and Replenish — this term is often thought of
as referring only to the having of children, and it does to some
extent. But the term can also mean to indicate the need for the
members of the family to render service and to give sweet love
to each other as well as to others in God's extended family.

Can you not sense in all of these great blessings the fact
that the Savior is so important to us? We are instructed to come
unto Christ and we are taught how to do that in the temple
ordinances — all of them. Even though our ultimate goal is to
come unto the Father, we cannot do that unless we come unto
Christ first and magnify the blessings of the temple covenants.

Chapter 1   85

In order to gain all of these blessings, the Lord has instructed us to serve Him with all our heart, might, mind, and strength (see Matthew 22:37 and D&C 4). If we succeed in attaining that level of service, it can then be said of us as it was said of Alma, Ammon, and Aaron, *" . . .And they were also distinguished for their zeal towards God, and also towards men; for they were perfectly honest and upright in all things; and they were firm in the faith of Christ, even unto the end."* (see Alma 27:27).

It is in this context, and only in this context, that the Savior will reveal and set forth all thrones, dominions, principalities, and powers as well as all of the other blessings of the temple ordinances not mentioned in this scripture (D&C 121:29).

86 Where Art Thou

Chapter Nine

FEW ARE CHOSEN

D&C 121:34 — "Behold, there are many called, but few are chosen. And why are they not chosen?"

Under ordinary circumstances, most of us would not stop reading this scripture at the end of this verse which consists of one profound statement followed by a disturbing question. With our curiosity aroused, we would move on to the next verse in order to obtain the answer to the Lord's question. However, it is the statement that bears much closer examination in this chapter.

Many are called, but few are chosen. Such a thought has probably caused a lot of people to wonder in their minds. We know that we are called but will we be chosen? Some perhaps will feel that by attempting to live the principles of the Gospel, they are depriving themselves of the "fun" experiences of life.

One of the most gratifying feelings that we can have in our daily existence is to possess the calm, peaceful assurance that we are in control of our own lives. When we have such beautiful feelings, we know what we are doing; we are relatively sure of the direction in which we are heading; and we feel loved and wanted by those who are important to us in our lives.

Now, a person who possesses such feelings has not sacrificed anything. True, he or she may not be having as much "fun" as measured by worldly standards, but that individual is experiencing a far deeper sense of happiness than those who grab at the straws thrown by Lucifer into the wind. Such happiness can obviously come to any individual in the world who refuses to believe that we only go around once so enjoy it while we can.

To those who are members of the Lord's true Church, however, much more is given and much more is expected. Why not? If we are given more truth and if we develop the deepest sense of love for our Heavenly Father, should not our feelings of calm, peaceful assurance be that much richer and yet cost that much more?

One prime example of this frequently shows up in the payment of tithing. Some pay it but think of what they could be using the money for if they were to not give it to the Church. Others fulfil the requirement of the law because they are totally convinced that this is the Lord's will and their commitment to their covenants is complete. They know they will be blessed but they give simply because they love the Lord, not for any return from God.

In this regard, the Lord knows that there will a goodly number who will not hold true to the greater knowledge and opportunity which He has provided for them. *"These are they who are not valiant in the testimony of Jesus; wherefore, they obtain not the crown over the kingdom of our God"* (see D&C 76:79). Paul reasoned the same way when he was describing those who were traitors, heady, highminded, or lovers of pleasures as *"having a form of godliness, but denying the power thereof: from such turn away"* (see 2 Timothy 3:5).

To know what we should turn away from requires concentrated search of the scriptures. However, quite often in studying the teachings of the Church we become familiar with certain passages of scripture. We use them or hear them so many times that the resultant familiarity causes us to look past

Chapter 1   89

a more profound meaning in them.

In order to explain that statement, we need to remember that when Joseph Smith was reading in the Book of James in the Holy Bible, he was doing it because he had attended a Methodist meeting and the minister had used that text in that meeting. He went home and studied it because he was confused. Ministers of other religions had used the same text but had ascribed different meanings to it.

You may recall that a part of his family were Methodists and another part were Presbyterian. He, himself, was undecided because of such confusing meanings given to the same verse of scripture by different ministers. How could that be so? He did not doubt the truthfulness of the Bible, only such interpretations.

The verse in James 1:5 deeply impressed him. It reads: *"If any of you lack wisdom, let him ask of God, that giveth to all men liberally, and upbraideth not; and it shall be given him."* He had previously selected the place to which he would go in order to ask in fervent prayer for divine assistance as to which church he should join. When the appropriate moment arrived, he then went to that place in that grove of trees to offer his prayer of faith. Note that he assumed that the true church was on the earth. Hence, his question pertained to which one was it!

Immediately, Joseph was set upon by Satan who inundated him with such a powerful feeling of blackness. It is interesting to note, also, that Lucifer bound Joseph's tongue so that he could not speak his prayer; therefore, he could not ask his question. It was a very real and frightening experience. There was nothing imaginary about it. Satan was there very quickly to stop this fourteen—year—old boy from asking such a simple question as to which church should he join.

We noted similar activities on the part of Lucifer in the mission field. Quite often, as soon as the missionaries began to teach the discussions to interested persons, ministers, who had never visited those people for many years, suddenly found reasons to make such visits. Many times, they brought with them pages and pages of anti—Mormon literature to speak against those teachings of the "Mormon" missionaries. Even relatives came after many months of absence to speak against the missionaries. It is fascinating to note the extent of the falsehoods perpetuated by such people who would go to any lengths to keep another individual out of the Lord's Church.

Elder Jeffrey Holland describes such reactions by Lucifer and those who listen to him as *"hardball time."* He refers to the experience of Joseph Smith in the Sacred Grove as one in which *"the gloves were off."* This game of hardball is still going on as Satan seeks to stop the work only it is us, rather than Joseph, who is on the court with him.

The Savior's response to Joseph's question was harsh yet so true and real. In his account of his experience, the words of the Lord were so indelibly imprinted on the boy's mind that he never forgot them. When he wrote the historical account of it some eighteen years later, he still was able to quote the Lord's words exactly as he had received them.

They are given in Joseph Smith — History 1:19 as a direct quote. *" . . .they draw near to me with their **lips**, but their **hearts** are far from me, they teach for doctrines the commandments of men, having a **form** of godliness, but they deny the **power** thereof."*

It is to this passage that reference was made earlier. We have heard it so often that we seem to pass over some important additional meanings. The overall message of the Savior was profoundly important. It referred to conditions in the Christian world when Joseph Smith was searching for the true church. It applied to "them."

But it also applies to us — yes, even to us in the Church today — those who have benefited from Joseph's inquiry.

Chapter 1   91

How is that? It is so because we need always to look at and keep in mind the Savior's choice of the words: **"lips—hearts"** and **"form—power."** In addition, the associations of these specific words are also important. In the English language, such combinations form parallels in meaning. If we forget the words and the associations, we will be in the same classification as those to whom the Savior referred when He was speaking to Joseph Smith on the memorable day. Perhaps an example of this might clarify it for us.

It has always been an interesting experience to sit on the beach and watch various individuals enter the ocean water. Some will wade in slowly and carefully. They gingerly feel their way into the water stopping at various times to allow their bodies to adjust to the temperature of the water. Sometimes they stop when they are knee—deep in the ocean and wait; others will move on until they are waist—deep, then wait, even stay. A few will wait for a while, then go on out until their shoulders are covered but their feet will still touch the floor of the ocean. Regardless of the reasoning behind their moves, these individuals demonstrate the "lips—form" illustration used by the Savior.

A smaller number of hardy individuals simply start running on the beach, head straight for the ocean, go as far on their feet as they can, splashing everyone in close proximity, then dive in head first to be totally immersed in the water. Regardless of their reasons, they go all the way at once. While you can argue the validity of these people's actions, the example is especially true when applied to those of us who are members of the Lord's true Church. Those who go all the way demonstrate the "hearts—power" part of the Savior's equation.

As we ponder on this opening of meaning to a scripture we have read and used often, we discover that the "lips—form" group of individuals have a number of similarities. However, it is not enough to just read about these. We have to be very sure that they are not a part of our own lives.

92   Where Art Thou

*They have form which enables them to look, speak, and act like good Church members but the power is missing. It is similar to having a very expensive automobile parked in your driveway but it is devoid of an engine. It looks great but it is worthless. Elder Neal A. Maxwell pointed to a similar analogy concerning disciples of Christ who "look good" but who are only going the motions in serving Christ. He wrote: "Discipleship is not simply surviving and enduring; discipleship is pressing forward, a creative Christianity. Discipleship does not wait to be acted upon, but instead acts upon men and circumstances to make things better" (see *Things As They Really Are*, p. 100).

*Some individuals frequently use their Church membership or the titles of their Church positions for their own selfish gain. It is not unusual to hear someone who is trying to sell you something or to involve you in some nefarious investment scheme tell you that he served as a bishop or in some other position, Fortunately, there are only a few of these people. Those who do this have form but no power. A suggestion is that you refuse to listen to such individuals because the Church's official position opposes such tactics.

*Some individuals never seem to get started in the Gospel. Some fall away after baptism. Others are going to get more involved tomorrow. Still others grab the iron rod but fall and rarely get up, frequently blaming the Lord for their own problems brought on by a lack of wisdom or devotion. Some even get to the end of the rod, taste of the fruit, but are ashamed and slip back into a more comfortable lifestyle in which there is less criticism from friends and family— a greater fear of men rather than a love for God. All of these examples include people who have form, but no power; or who give lip service to their membership, but not their hearts.

*This is the hypocrite who always talks a better game than he plays. He frequently is heard to advise others to do as he says, not as he does — a psychological device used to put a

Chapter 1   93

soothing ointment on his own feelings of guilt. In reality, such individuals do not believe anywhere near as much as they say they do. Their knowledge of the Gospel is usually very shallow and their power to control their righteous actions is even more empty.

*Individuals who have form but no power are similar to those described by President Spencer W. Kimball in that *"they are forever stringing and unstringing the instrument while the song they came to sing remains unsung."*

*Such individuals are as soldiers ordered into combat. They show up in their dress uniforms ready for the party when all the time they needed to wear their combat fatigues and to carry their weapons. Notice, for example, how few members really use, or even bring, their scriptures to Church or who flounder badly when asked to look up a reference such as Jarom, Enos, and so on.

The above is not intended to show despair. Nor is it intended to criticize any member of the Church. There is no intention to judge anyone. All that is intended is to point out observations of the actions noted over the years of some people who have lips—form memberships and to use these actions as guides for our own behavior patterns. We simply must do better. The place to start is to be sure we do not have form without power in our lives, and that we are not guilty of an empty lip service type of "devotion" to Christ.

Better still, we need to eliminate the concept of lips— form entirely from our lives and concentrate on the hearts— power equation as given by our Savior. In keeping with this, those members who have hearts—power reflect certain great and admirable qualities.

*They are champions who push themselves into agony because they know that there is a pain barrier in every race and by going through that barrier they will find the last few meters that wins the race. Roger Bannister almost gave

94   Where Art Thou

up before he reached that pain barrier but he persisted and paid
the price. As a result, he became the first human being to run
a mile in under four minutes — a feat that has been now
matched by many, but never duplicated.

***These are those members who grab hold of the iron
rod very firmly, stay with it regardless of problems, and
make it to the end, overcoming all trials and tribulations
along the way.** In addition, by so enduring, they strengthen
and increase their natural capabilities as well as find new ones
they never thought they had.

***Often, such people are the unsung heroes of the
Church whose actions and lives never become known
except to a few.** They seek no publicity and beat no drums.
One choice example of this are those men and women — often
in their seventies, eighties, even nineties — who devote many
hours as proxies in the temples and who can always be trusted
to be there. Without such people, the pace of the work being
performed for the dead would have faltered years ago.

***These are they who truly realize that there is no such
thing as cheap grace and that, while the Lord stands at the
door, it is we who must open that door and do His work.** Look,
for example, at the fact that all of the great revelations received
by Joseph Smith and other Prophets of the latter days came
because they inquired of the Lord. They experienced a concern;
they did something about it; and they received an answer.

***Members who have hearts and power are those who
are truly converted to the Gospel of Jesus Christ;** who serve
faithfully and loyally without questions about revelation and
inspiration; and who do not need to be supervised every
moment of every day as they carry out those things that they
have promised to do. A few unwise individuals refer to such
devotion as blind obedience, and use that term in a negative
way as if to say that such faithful performance is given in much
the same way that a dog serves his master. In reality, people

Chapter 1　　　　　　　　　　95

who have hearts and power are truly converted to the Laws of
Consecration, Sacrifice, and Obedience. They do not have to
debate internally when the clarion call comes from the Lord
through His servants. They have mentally made the commitment first. Thereafter, there is never any need to debate the call
or the required actions to fulfil it.

There are three ways in which we can overcome our natural
man tendency to do "lips—form" service and to become true
spiritual giants yearning to serve with our "hearts—power"
capabilities and commitments. These are described below.

1. Do everything you possibly can to increase and heighten
your **sensitivity to spiritual matters.** This is done by re-
questing in faith those gifts of the Holy Ghost that you need as
a part of your powers of heaven. You should particularly think
about asking the Lord to bless you with discernment, wisdom,
faith to heal and be healed, and understanding. You must keep
your spiritual edge very sharp and in focus or your picture of
life becomes blurred and lost.

2. Request in your prayers and by your daily living
practices **enhanced endowments of power.** These include
your abilities to learn, to teach, to recall, to love, and to edify.
To have such endowments in your life will fulfil for you
personally what the Lord wants for the whole Church, *"And
now, behold, I give unto you a commandment, that when* (1)
*ye shall instruct and edify each other, that ye may know how
to* (2) *act and direct my church,* (3) *how to act upon the points
of my law and commandments which I have given. And thus* (4)
ye shall become instructed in the law of my church, and (5) *be
sanctified by that which ye have received, and* (6) *ye shall bind
yourselves to act in all holiness before me"* (see D&C 43:8—9).

3. Pray for and receive **communion with ministering
angels** because you are entitled to heavenly help by virtue of
your faithful living. Moroni tells us that *"by the ministering of
angels, and by every word which proceedeth forth out of the*

mouth of God, men began to exercise faith in Christ; and thus by faith, they did lay hold of every good thing; and thus it was until the coming of Christ." Then Moroni asks: *"Or have angels ceased to appear unto the children of men? Or has he withheld the power of the Holy Ghost from them? Or will he, so long as time shall last, or the earth shall stand, or there shall be one man upon the face thereof to be saved?"* (see Moroni 7:36).

In the same chapter, this great prophet, who saw the events of our day so clearly, asks that same question three times, thus giving emphasis to a critical value that we should have in our lives. He instructs us that the office of their [ministering angels] ministry is to (a) call men unto repentance; (b) to fulfil and do the work of the covenants of the Father; and (c) to prepare the way among the children of men, by declaring the word of Christ unto the chosen vessels of the Lord, that they may bear testimony of him (see Moroni 7:31).

There is one additional concept that accompanies the above stated idea about helping oneself first. It is beautifully developed by Moroni when he was describing the events surrounding the demise of the Jaredites because of their exceeding wickedness. He refers to the faith exercised by such great men as Moses, Alma, Amulek, Nephi, Lehi, Ammon, the brother of Jared, and the three Nephites.

In each instance, Moroni demonstrates the fact that these men had exercised their faith first, then they were free to ask for and were eligible to receive marvelous spiritual experiences. *"And now, I, Moroni, would speak somewhat concerning these things; I would show unto the world that faith is things which are hoped for and not seen; wherefore, dispute not because ye see not, for ye receive no witness until after the trial of your faith"* (see Ether 12:6).

Once these great men had each individually passed that trial of faith test, they were rewarded with personal revelations of the type that are reserved for the chosen vessels of the Lord.

Chapter 1   97

We then read, *"And there were many whose faith was so exceedingly strong, even before Christ came, who could not be kept from within the veil, but truly saw with their eyes the things which they had beheld with an eye of faith, and they were glad"* (see Ether 12:19).

You are the chosen vessel of the Lord. You can receive great and continuing help from ministering angels if and when you need it and if and when you ask for it. Your motives have to be righteous and pure. You must have tried to have helped yourself first. The injunction, then, requires you to ask: then you will receive.

The chosen vessels of the Lord will always include you as long as you are working to be chosen. You certainly have been called to His service. To remain chosen, you must use your **heart** to move past and beyond mere **lip** service and you must look through and go around the **forms** of men's philosophies and selfish, natural—man desires. If you do that, you will turn on your full divinely installed **power.** *"But behold, that which is of God inviteth and enticeth to do good continually; wherefore, every thing which inviteth and enticeth to do good, and to love God, and to serve him, is inspired of God"* (see Moroni 7:13). Hence, you will be both called and chosen.

98 Where Art Thou

Chapter Ten

THEY DO NOT LEARN THIS ONE LESSON

D&C 121:35 — "Because their hearts are set so much upon the things of this world, and aspire to the honors of men, that they do not learn this one lesson —"

Again we have an incomplete scripture that is easy to read over very quickly. When reading verses 34 to 36 of D&C 121, we are prone to place emphasis on verses 34 and 36 and overlook verse 35. If we do this, we will be missing the important message in the first part of this particular verse. It is that we can choose our aspirations and courses of actions.

The one principle of truth that is at the very core of God's dealings with all of His children everywhere is that of free agency. It was this principle that caused our Father to select Jesus Christ to be our Savior for Lucifer would have controlled us in such a way that not one of us would have been lost. At the same time, he wanted all of the glory and all of the credit for forcing us back into Heaven. In Satan's plans, there was no need for us to have the freedom to choose. Our final place of arrival would have been pre—destined.

Therein lies one of our greatest problems and misconceptions. We have come to equate any infringement upon our free agency with force. In reality, we need to equate free agency with responsibility, but we often tend to overlook this relationship, because it is convenient to justify our actions at that particular moment.

In order to fully appreciate the proper equation, and therefore this scripture, we need to comprehend the eternal principle of free agency. Then, we have to understand how our perceptions either add to or take away from the responsibility of our free agency.

Frequently when we think of free agency or freedom, our first thoughts usually go to our political rights or our personal liberties. Unfortunately, either of these, and both of them, assume short—termed, temporary status, mostly because of how we develop them. For example, our personal liberties include our bodily appetites, the application of which is the cause of many of our transgressions against the Word of Wisdom and the Laws of Chastity, Obedience, Sacrifice, and Consecration.

No one is daring to say that political and personal freedoms are unimportant. They are fundamental to our existence when accompanied by a full recognition and acceptance of the responsibilities that must go along with them. It is this that is often ignored in our selfishness and pride.

There is a third freedom that is even more important to us as children of God. It is more enduring than other freedoms, and it embraces the two freedoms already discussed when applied to its greatest and fullest extent. This third freedom is our moral or spiritual one. It is given to us so that we can decided for ourselves what type of a person we really want to become, and then to select the process by which we will develop the character required by that type of chosen person.

Lehi, in blessing his son Jacob, spoke of the Messiah and how He would redeem mankind from the fall of Adam and Eve. He stated that because " . . .*they are redeemed from the fall they have become free forever, knowing good from evil; to*

Chapter 1   101

act for themselves and not to be acted upon, . . . " (see 2 Nephi 2:26).

It was then, and it still is, the Lord's intention that we act for ourselves in all phases and activities of our lives. The most important of these are the spiritual relationships and responsibilities which we have to our Heavenly Father, to our families, and to ourselves.

What we have to realize is that we do have the freedom to accept or reject the making of a covenant with God. If we exercise that right and make that covenant, we no longer have the freedom of choice as to whether or not we will obey the conditions and requirements of that covenant.

Having made it, we now have the responsibility of obeying and living up to the requirements of that covenant if we want to receive the associated blessings. Yes, we can ignore that covenant but that is not free agency — it is plain and simple transgression. If we do not live up to the conditions and requirements, we can only expect to receive the punishment(s). This is because we have not invoked free agency but the Laws of Mercy and Justice. The freedom to choose was ours to begin with; it cannot be used again as an excuse to cover up or justify the breaking of our promises to the Lord.

The biggest single roadblock to learning in God's way as well as to wisely handling our free agency is that of our own personal perceptions. These either promote, or interfere with, our understanding of correct principles, our day—to—day relationships with other human beings, and our interdependent interactions with each member of the Godhead.

It is incumbent upon each and every one of us to study this subject of perceptions. Many a friendship has been damaged; quite a few marriages have resulted in divorce; hundreds of sins have been excused; and thousands of angry words have been exchanged because of misperceptions. Had we examined our perceptions more deeply, and reflected carefully for even a few moments, we could have frequently reduced the quantity of such reactions. We could have, also, substantially increased the quality of our relationships with others, especially those who are most significant to us.

Given such behavior patterns, it would be appropriate if a few basic concepts are presented in this chapter. These could serve as a basis for your more detailed and thorough study of both free agency and perceptions because they are inter—related.

Your brain records everything that involves any one or any combination of your five senses. These serve as collection or gathering devices. No attempt is made by the brain to determine the accuracy, completeness, or appropriateness of these pieces of information which are accumulated during this continuous gathering process.

A number of items of gathered information will be summarily rejected because they are offensive to your values or because you simply refuse to consider them. The largest amount of information, however, will be retained in your brain's storage cells, and very likely, new learnings will be associated with something you already have learned in the past and categorized into groups. This is a subconscious procedure.

The problems, that we experience, begin when we almost always automatically assume that all of our perceptions are correct. This occurs because we are convinced that we are the only ones who see the world as it really is. Therefore, the way that others see it has to be wrong when it conflicts with ours. Having automatically made that assumption, we proceed to act out our perceptions. However, because it is subconscious, it can cause serious problems.

For example, if you had attended a presentation of Handel's "Messiah" on a previous occasion, that experience is now a part of your subconscious mind. Then, upon reading of another presentation of the same musical, your mind would

Chapter 1

assume that it would be a very similar production and all that you would have to do, when you arrive at the concert hall, is to sit back and enjoy it. In reality, however, if you had not read the advanced publicity very thoroughly, you would not have taken your own musical score to the performance with you. This prevents you from participating with the audience in the chorus numbers of the production.

While this example is not so critical, you can probably remember others from your own experiences that were much more serious. The only way we can avoid such difficulties in our lives is for us to make ourselves read or listen to details more carefully and thoroughly. When we are too ready to accept our mind's associations of new experiences with previously acquired ones, we assume that we have heard, seen, or acted out that before. In reality, this may be far from the truth.

In fact, we are so convinced that we see the reality of the world so clearly and correctly, that we usually proceed to act out our perceptions without questioning them. We will base our current and future experiences, shape our present and future attitudes, and formulate our on—going and forthcoming dealings with others on those perceptions. We will most likely not even permit ourselves to admit that some of our perceptions may indeed be wrong. Not every "ah—ha" experience will result in such an admission, even though most "ah—ha" experiences shed new light on our perceptions. "Ah—ha" experiences occur to us when a new concept, or a different interpretation of a previously learned idea, opens up new understandings to our minds.

The interesting fact is that, even when we do recognize that our perceptions are wrong, we first seek to justify or rationalize them rather than to correct or completely change them. The reason we respond in this manner is because we refuse to see the world as other people perceive it. Hence, we would rather conclude that they are insincere, uninformed, selfish, or out of touch. The so—called generation gap is one

104   Where Art Thou

example of these kinds of reactions. They undoubtedly lead to great difficulties in credibility, personality, and communication.

If we develop the skill we need to listen properly and fully to others, we may sympathize or even empathize with others. However, sympathy and empathy may be inappropriate responses at that time to that person's problems. It is seldom that we will truly listen to understand the feelings of others. When we listen to really understand, we have to do so without selfish inhibitions and agendas of our own, because we just may have to be the ones who must change our own ideas and behaviors.

You see, there is one inescapable fact that you must comprehend. It is that your perceptions direct and control your behavior. If your perceptions are correct, your behavior will be correspondingly correct. Conversely, if your perceptions are incorrect, your behavior will be a source of great and continuing problems to you until you change the incorrect perceptions.

In order to clarify these concepts, here are a few points for you to consider. In effect, they summarize what we have already discussed.

*Your perceptions are continually being added to and modified as you admit new pieces of information gathered by your collection devices — your five senses.

*These perceptions control your values, attitudes, and behaviors.

*You will retain all of those pieces of information that match your existing beliefs and curiosities. You will be even more certain that you are understanding Gospel truths, human interactions, and other concepts or principles as they really are. In your mind, you will be convinced that you are grasping reality.

*When you open your mouth to express yourself, you will be frequently describing your own biases, prejudices, and

Chapter 1   105

beliefs. You will not be willing to substantially reduce these problems until you train and make yourself see the world as it is, rather than how you think it is.

*Unless corrected, errors in your perceptions will continually cause you problems in credibility, personality, and communication, To overcome these difficulties you must learn to:

1. Listen to understand others instead of listening to defend your own point of view. Avoid uncalled—for sympathy or unnecessary empathy.

2. Speak to be understood rather than to polarize the issues. Instead of saying, "you don't understand," say "let me see if I understand what you are telling me."

3. Find a common point of agreement when differences exist in important situations, especially if you do not totally or even partially agree. Use those common points to formulate a new solution that all parties can accept.

4. Train yourself to see not with your eye but with your soul.

5. Look for meaning, not for differences. Refrain from invoking your own personal defense mechanisms.

6. Remember that a solution to a problem is not a solution if it does not change the perception(s) that created the problem. Such a resolution may not be an either—or solution. It may require moving to new ground so that both parties emerge as winners, even though total agreement was not reached.

In addition to the above listed six steps, there is one more very important problem that each of us has to solve regarding the thoughts that we have accumulated in our minds as perceptions. It is that many individuals think that they can indulge in looking at indecent pictures or movies, or in listening to impure jokes, musical lyrics, or dialogue, and emerge untouched or unchanged.

In reality, every experience that these individuals have ever had with obscenity is recorded in their brains waiting to be recalled when the appropriate stimulus is received. Quite often, this happens at the most inopportune moments, which can be embarrassing, to say the least. Until changed, these experiences will always be there.

Later in life, when the love of the Savior becomes a strong focal point in their lives, these individuals acquire a burning desire to erase these obscenities. When this level of spiritualized thinking is reached, the question then becomes one of knowing how to effect the desired changes.

One sure process is to change the undesirable thought at the exact moment that it is recalled to the conscious part of the mind. In order to be ready, it is suggested that the individual keep in his or her possession ten to twelve small cards, on each of which is written one clean, beautiful thought, scripture, or verse. As soon as the undesirable thought comes to mind, the person whips out the cards, reads and ponders any one of the thoughts, thereby substituting [or recording over] the unwanted one. Do not become discouraged if you use this technique. It is a thought—for—thought exchange process. You may have the same unwanted thought stored several times in your mind. Each one has to be replaced individually.

Another excellent method is to use an "Affirmation Card." An example is given below. On it, write one **specific** affirmation that you want to acquire or change. Be sure that the affirmation is attainable. Examples would be: "I will make my daily prayers an interview with God"; or "I will eliminate all unclean thoughts from my mind."

Write your affirmation on line number 1. After that is done, look at it carefully, ponder its meaning and value to you, incorporate it into your thinking process. The second day, you

Chapter 1

107

write down the **exact same affirmation** on line 2, and then repeat the thinking process. This procedure is followed for **twenty—one consecutive days**. If you miss a day, you must start over again by commencing a new day 1.

```
┌──────────────────────────────┬──────────────────────────────┐
│      AFFIRMATION CARD         │ 11 _____   │
│ 1 _____    │ 12 _____   │
│ 2 _____    │ 13 _____   │
│ 3 ___                         │ 14 _____   │
│ 4 ___                         │ 15 _____   │
│ 5 ___                         │ 16 _____   │
│ 6 ___                         │ 17 _____   │
│ 7 ___                         │ 18 _____   │
│ 8 _____    │ 19 _____   │
│ 9 _____    │ 20 _____   │
│ 10 _____    │ 21 _____   │
└──────────────────────────────┴──────────────────────────────┘
```

When you follow this affirmation card procedure, you will experience a number of strange feelings during the first ten to twelve days. The process requires you to undergo a substantial change in your thinking and in your actions. At first, your mind will resist the proposed change(s). You will be subconsciously tempted to return to the "old way," because it is easier and less troublesome to your conscience. You will have strong, powerful urges to take the path of least resistance.

But, if you have courage, faith, and integrity, you will work your way through these Satanistic—inspired resistances. You must keep your goal firmly entrenched in your mind. It would help you greatly if you take out your affirmation card as many times a day as necessary in order to renew your commitment and courage, and subdue the resistance.

108   Where Art Thou

Make up your own affirmation card. Once you have completed the twenty—one day process, begin again with another affirmation, but work on only one at a time. It is of invaluable help if you put a picture of the Savior on your card so that you can frequently remind yourself of His loving and cleansing grace. Using this card will truly assist you in putting your spiritual values in perspective and of primary importance in your life.

When our hearts are set so much upon the things of this world, and when we aspire to the honors of men, we need to definitively examine our commitment to the God—given and preserved principle of free agency. No other Gospel principle has been so dedicatedly preserved unto us by our Father in Heaven and His Son, Jesus Christ. For this principle, He was selected to be our Savior and Redeemer.

We also need to develop our understanding of how our perceptions impact on our lifestyles. The Lord outlined for us an excellent guide for us to use, *"Behold, you have not understood* [a perception problem]; *you have supposed that I would give it unto you, when you took no thought save it was to ask me* [free agency problem]. *But, behold, I say unto you, that you must study it out in your mind* [correction of perception problem]; *then you must ask me if it be right, and if it is right I will cause that your bosom shall burn within you* [reality]; *therefore, you shall feel that it is right. But if it be not right, you shall have no such feelings, but you shall have a stupor of thought that shall cause you to forget the thing which is wrong* [free agency] . . ." (see D&C 9:7).

Without free agency, we could always be with God through His grace, but we could never become like God through our own efforts and the Savior's mercy. Unless we follow Alma's advice to his son Corianton, our false perceptions and our abuse of our free agency will always be at the root of our pursuit of worldly things and honors. Neither will we ever rise to the quality level of godliness and personal goodness required of a candidate for Exaltation in the Celes-

Chapter 1

tial Kingdom. *"Suffer not yourself to be led away by any vain or foolish thing; suffer not the devil to lead away your heart again . . ."* (see Alma 39:11).

110   Where Art Thou

Chapter Eleven

RIGHTS OF THE PRIESTHOOD

D&C 121: 36 —"*That the rights of the priesthood are inseparably connected with the powers of heaven, and that the powers of heaven cannot be controlled nor handled only upon the principles of righteousness.***"**

You are asked to read this scripture again very carefully. It is very important that you realize the three key elements as well as the sequence of those elements. The three elements are **"rights of the priesthood," "powers of heaven,"** and **"principles of righteousness."** When we speak of these three elements, we are referring to the entire plan of our Heavenly Father from the creation in the pre—existence of His spirit children to His giving of the final reward to us. Hence, the great importance of understanding of both the elements and the sequence.

The scripture states that the **rights of the priesthood** are connected to the **powers of heaven** and that you cannot control these powers except on the **principles of righteousness**. Therefore, the correct sequence is as follows: (1) **rights of the priesthood**; (2) **principles of righteousness**; (3) **powers of heaven**. This sequence is often missed by many when glossing over the scripture. As we develop and define each of these three elements, you will realize why the correct sequence is so important.

112   Where Art Thou

The first element is the **rights of the priesthood**. These rights are the keys, covenants, and authority pertaining to the priesthood offices which are necessary for the conduct of the Lord's work and for the exaltation of all men and women. This has always been so, and it will always remain so.

Joseph Smith stated that *"the priesthood was first given to Adam; he obtained the First Presidency and held the keys from generation to generation, He obtained it in the creation, before the world was formed"* . . ."*The priesthood is an everlasting principle and existed with God from eternity and will to eternity, without beginning of days or end of years"* (see *Teachings of the Prophet Joseph Smith*, p. 157).

Elder Bruce R. McConkie instructed us that *"the priesthood is the power and authority to* ***act*** *(upon which verb I place emphasis) to* ***act*** *in all things pertaining to the salvation of men. It is the means whereby the Lord acts through men to save souls."* (Regional Representatives' Seminar, 4 October 1973).

Inasmuch as the priesthood is an everlasting principle, and, since it is the power to act in all things pertaining to the salvation of men, it naturally follows that the **rights of the priesthood** include all keys and covenants. Without these, we could not act in all things because it requires the keys and covenants to prepare all of us for Exaltation. If only one key had not been restored, a significant part of the work could not be done. This, then, would most certainly not be the Dispensation of the Fulness of Times.

Baptism opens the door to the Celestial Kingdom. It is the beginning step in a series of critical covenants that we need to experience in order to reach our greatest potential and receive our greatest reward. Yet, despite its importance, we cannot become sons and daughters, and, therefore, heirs of our Eternal Family simply by being baptized, after we have repented of our sins. It takes much more than that.

Chapter 1   113

```
┌──────┬──────────┬──────────────────────────┐
│  B   │  GIFT    │  RIGHTS OF THE           │
│  A   │   OF     │  PRIESTHOOD              │
│  P   │  THE     ├──────────────────────────┤
│      │          │  (KEYS AND COVENANTS     │
│  T   │  HOLY    │  PERTAINING TO PRIEST-   │
│  I   │  GHOST   │  HOOD OFFICES AND        │
│      │          │  BLESSINGS.)             │
│  S   │          ├──────────────────────────┤
│      │          │  AUTHORITY               │
│  M   │          │                          │
│      │          │  ORDINATION-POWER        │
│      │          │  KEYS TO PRESIDE         │
│      │          │  INITIATORY ORDINANCES   │
│      │          │                          │
│      │          │  OBEDIENCE               │
│      │          │  SACRIFICE               │
│      │          │  VIRTUE                  │
│      │          │  GOSPEL PRINCIPLES       │
│      │          │  CONSECRATION            │
│      │          │  ETERNAL MARRIAGE        │
└──────┴──────────┴──────────────────────────┘
```

President Joseph F. Smith stated that, *"to become the sons and daughters of God, children and heirs of God, and joint—heirs with Christ, we must suffer with him, that we may be glorified with him. In other words, we must receive in our hearts, accept in our hearts, every principle of the gospel which has been revealed; and insofar as it is our power to do so, we must live in accordance with these principles and keep the commandments of God in full"* (see *Gospel Doctrine*, p. 140).

Having been baptized, we are then permitted to have one, who holds the proper priesthood authority, lay his hands upon our head and bestow the Holy Ghost upon us. This is very important to us because it is through the Holy Ghost that we receive a testimony of the divinity of Jesus Christ, His mission, and our individual roles in that mission. When properly used by us, the Holy Ghost will indeed be a constant companion to us in revealing, inspiring, warning, and protecting us as

114   Where Art Thou

we work our way through this life.

To enter Exaltation, however, we need the **rights of the priesthood**. The Lord has given unto us privileges, blessings, an opportunity to enter into sacred covenants, and the invitation to accept ordinances that pertain to our salvation far beyond what is preached by the world and its ministers. These great rights carry us very vividly into an understanding of the principles of faith in the Lord Jesus Christ, repentance from sin, baptism by immersion for the remission of sins, and the laying on of hands for the gift of the Holy Ghost. In saying these things in this way, we, in no way, diminish the critical importance that each of these basic principles of the Gospel have for us.

These privileges and covenants are received nowhere else but in the temple of God. That is why they carry us beyond the fundamentals mentioned in the preceding paragraph. Elder Joseph Fielding Smith instructed us that, *"The ordinances of the temple, the endowment and sealings, pertain to exaltation in the celestial kingdom, where the sons and daughters are. Sons and daughters have access to the home where they dwell, and you cannot receive that access until you go to the temple. Why? Because you must receive certain key words as well as make covenants by which you are able to enter. If you try to get into the house, and the door is locked, how are you going to enter, if you haven't your key? You get your key in the temple, which will admit you"* (see *Doctrine of Salvation*, 2:40).

Every construction expert uses blueprints to build any type of project. Such plans outline the instructions he needs pertaining to the size of the project, the material to be used, and the appearance of the final product. In His wisdom, the Lord knows that we need a similar blueprint for our daily living, and He placed it in the temple for us to discover. The ordinances performed therein, and the associated instruction which is given, provide us with a full plan by which we must live in order to accomplish what Joseph Fielding Smith said — enter into the House of our Father through the proper door. That plan is our blueprint.

Chapter 1   115

Such a critical concept is worth restating because it seems to be easily or conveniently forgotten by many. To enter Exaltation, we need and must have the **rights of the priesthood** as manifested in the higher ordinances of the Gospel as found only in the temple. These include the authority and power of the Melchizedek Priesthood and the initiatory, endowment, and sealing ordinances as outlined by the Savior to be taught in His holy house. Specific details are too sacred to discuss here, but references are given to some of the promises and covenants in this publication.

It has been wondered by some as to the origin of these temple ceremonies. A few seem to feel that the Prophet Joseph Smith borrowed many of the wordings and procedures from other groups. If you have similar feelings, you are exhorted to fast and pray for your own testimony. Remember: ask and it shall be given unto you, seek and ye shall find. Once you have paid the price, there will no longer be any doubt in your mind. These sacred ordinances and covenants came from no earthly source. They are from the Lord by way of divine revelation to the latter—day Prophets of God.

One additional thought is necessary concerning the keys and the authority of the priesthood. You may have the authority to perform an ordinance, but you cannot do it until you are duly authorized by the one who holds the proper keys. For example, a man cannot ordain his son to the Aaronic Priesthood just because he is the father and an Elder. He has to be authorized by the Bishop, who holds the keys of the Aaronic Priesthood in that ward.

In our scripture from D&C 121:36, quoted at the beginning of this chapter, we are told that the **rights of the priesthood** are inseparably connected to the **powers of heaven**. What is that connection? It is that the keys and covenants of the priesthood are bestowed upon us conditionally here on this earth. The condition is that we prove ourselves worthy and faithful and obedient in all things.

116 Where Art Thou

It is encumbant upon us to *act*. We cannot make those covenants which are included in the **rights of the priesthood** and then rest on our laurels. We cannot simply do nothing more than to go to the temple once for our own endowment. Nor can we safeguard our covenants by putting them away in a shoe box on the top shelf of a closet, never to use them for fear of losing them.

We must constantly exercise and expand on the **rights of the priesthood** with which we have been blessed. It is absolutely critical that we keep these rights constantly in our view and on our minds. One great scientist, Henry B. Eyring used to ask his son: *"What do you think about when you have nothing to think about?"* May we suggest that, when such moments occur, and they do, you think about your sacred covenants. You will draw much closer to Jesus Christ, and, as you so ponder, He will become your Friend as well as your Savior in a very personal relationship.

As mentioned earlier, these covenants and blessings are conditional. It will not be until the Lord Jesus Christ receives us into Exaltation in the Celestial Kingdom that our keys and covenants and blessings will be made permanent. Will there be any chance of deceiving Him?

Nephi gives us a very clear answer to that question. He wrote: *"O then, my beloved brethren, come unto the Lord, the Holy One. Remember that his paths are righteous. Behold, the way for man is narrow, but it lieth in a straight course before him, and the keeper of the gate is the Holy One of Israel; and he employeth no servant there; and there is none other way save it be by the gate; for he cannot be deceived, for the Lord God is his name"* (see 2 Nephi 9:41).

To reinforce the importance of the **rights of the priesthood**, we need to understand what the Lord said when the Twelve had met in council and were confessing their individual weaknesses as well as seeking divine guidance. They had repented of their sins, but they were soon to depart on missions for which they needed much help. *"The power and authority of the higher, or Melchizedek Priesthood, is to hold the keys of all the spiritual*

Chapter 1   117

blessings of the church — To have the privilege of receiving the mysteries of the kingdom of heaven, to have the heavens opened unto them, to commune with the general assembly and church of the Firstborn, and to enjoy the communion and presence of God the Father, and Jesus the mediator of the new covenant." (see D&C 107:18—19).

It has always been an interesting and curious concept as to why the Prophet Joseph Smith interjected the **principles of righteousness** in between the **rights of the priesthood** and the **powers of heaven**. It is also rather thought—provoking as to how the Prophet structured that sentence because a casual reading would most likely result in the reader missing the complicated sequence intended by Joseph Smith. A simple experiment in most Church classes would demonstrate that.

However, once we clarify the correct sequence, we can begin to realize what is meant by the term — **principles of righteousness**. In a revealing and beautiful explanation, Peter stated, *"According as his divine power hath given unto us all things that pertain unto life and godliness, through the knowledge of him that hath called us to glory and virtue; whereby are given unto us exceeding great and precious promises: that by these ye might be partakers of the divine nature."* (see 2 Peter 1:3—4).

Peter is so instructive in this writing. He tells us that we should clearly recognize that the Lord's divine power is given to us in such depth and magnitude that we have everything we need to attain godliness, glory, virtue, and a knowledge of Him. How else can we be partakers of the divine nature?

Why would we want to possess these blessings if we were not inclined to be partakers of the divine nature? What else do we have to do? Peter makes it very plain that we must be partakers of the divine nature. He leaves us with very little doubt concerning that task. What else, then, has the Lord given to us to help us achieve such a blessing and status?

The answer, of course, is in the **rights of the priesthood**,

Where Art Thou

which we have already discussed, and in the **powers of heaven**, which we have yet to discuss. However, there is a most fundamental step that must occur in between these, without which neither of these would mean much. That is why the **principles of righteousness** were placed in the middle of these other two concepts.

```
PRINCIPLES OF RIGHTEOUSNESS

(CHRIST-LIKE ATTRIBUTES)

FAITH                  GODLINESS
CHARITY                LOVE
VIRTUE                 KNOWLEDGE
TEMPERANCE             PATIENCE
BROTHERLY KINDNESS     HUMILITY
DILIGENCE              POWER
JUSTICE                JUDGMENT
MERCY                  TRUTH
SUBMISSIVENESS         MEEKNESS
```

As a result of His royal birthright, the Savior's nature included the human attributes of His mortal mother and the divine attributes of His Father. Thus, he had to grow from grace to grace, until He received a fulness of the Father's power. He was not excused from acquiring these principles, as we are not excused either. Just as He had to grow in personal ways, so His example must be ours. There are no substitutes for His attributes.

We are to be partakers of the divine nature — an act that is only possible if we understand that the **rights of the priesthood** teaches and motivates us to acquire the **principles of righteousness**.

Chapter 1   119

As we acquire these, the Lord opens up the windows of heaven and pours out the gifts and rewards referred to as the **powers of heaven**. That is why the sequencing of Joseph Smith's reasoning is so important. It is step one before step two, and steps one and two before step three.

The **principles of righteousness** thus assume great importance to us. It would be to your everlasting benefit to understand them very thoroughly. Because of that, we will discuss them in depth in Chapter Thirteen of this publication. You can obtain a preview of most of them from 1 Peter 1:5—7 and D&C 4:5—6. As you study them, you are urged to strive to understand how tightly interwoven these principles are to our perceptions. The fact is, we must be constantly changing our perceptions as we become much more Christ—like when acquiring His attributes. We cannot try to change the attributes to match our perceptions.

The relationship of these **principles of righteousness** to the **rights of the priesthood** was very pointedly given by the Lord when He instructed us regarding the decisions of the First Presidency, The Twelve Apostles, and the Quorum of the Seventy: *"The decisions of these quorums, or either of them, are to be made in all righteousness, in holiness, and lowliness of heart, meekness and long suffering, and in faith, and virtue, and knowledge, temperance, patience, godliness, brotherly kindness and charity; because the promise is, if these things abound in them they shall not be unfruitful in the knowledge of the Lord"* (see D&C 107:30—31). Note that all decisions made by the presiding priesthood quorums of the Church are to be made using the **principles of righteousness** — first the priesthood and then the principles.

We have now discussed D&C 121:36 to the point of understanding the first two great elements given to us by our far—seeing Prophet Joseph Smith. We have also looked at how these two elements inter—relate and interact. We now need to examine the **powers of heaven** — the third concept in our sequence.

You should reflect upon previously made comments concerning the tendency that some people have to mix the **principles of righteousness** and the **powers of heaven**. There are clear—cut differences between these two concepts, and, while they work very closely together, they should not be confused. It would be very difficult to be blessed with the **powers of heaven** if we have not moved definitively towards becoming much more Christ—like through the acquisition of His attributes. The motivation for doing that should come from our experiences in the temple.

There is a very profound reason for keeping these two elements separate. It is that the Christ—like attributes are critically important personal qualities that we have to understand, then acquire. By keeping them separated, we can place them in much sharper focus. Without them we can never fulfil the Lord's words, *"The disciple is not above his master: but every one that is perfect shall be as his master."* (see Luke 6:40).

There is no way we can even begin to be as our Master without our acquisition of His attributes. The burden for doing that is on our shoulders. We have to want to acquire them, then we have to go to work to earn them. This is most definitely an action process that is placed on us, and there are no short cuts. Without definite signs of progress from us, the Lord cannot open up the windows of heaven as has been promised.

As soon as we are making substantial personal progress in that direction, we can feel free to *request* the gifts of God which constitute the **powers of heaven**. Those gifts, which are listed on the left hand side of the diagram are gifts of the Holy Ghost. The list is not

Chapter 1   121

complete but it is indicative of the gifts that are available to us. They will be bestowed upon us by that member of the Godhead if we are worthy, as well as when we have a specific need associated with a calling in the Church. The latter bestowal, however, is temporary and, when we are released, they are recalled. What we are interested in is a permanent bestowal of these gifts based on our personal worthiness.

From Moroni we learn, *" . . .that ye deny not the gifts of God, for they are many; and they come from the same God. And there are different ways that these gifts are administered; but it is the same God who worketh all in all; and they are given by the manifestations of the Spirit of God unto men, to profit them."* (see Moroni 10:8).

In the next eight verses, Moroni lists a number of these gifts or powers. Then he states: *"And all these gifts come by the Spirit of Christ; and they come unto every man severally, according as he will"* (see Moroni 10:17). It is interesting to note that the term "Spirit of Christ" as used by Moroni refers to the Holy Ghost through whom the Savior operates in bestowing these gifts. The listing on the next page will itemize these wonderful powers both as to the present and the future.

The Lord gave us virtually the same instruction in D&C 46:10—29. He then concludes by saying, *"He that asketh in the Spirit asketh according to the will of God; wherefore it is done even as he asketh. And again, I say unto you, all things must be done in the name of Christ, whatsoever you do in the Spirit; and ye must give thanks unto God in the Spirit for whatsoever blessing ye are blessed with. And ye must practise virtue and holiness before me continually . . . "* (see D&C 46:30—33).

From these scriptures we learn about some of the spiritual gifts which constitute some of the **powers of heaven**. We are also informed about how they operate. We can comprehend that such gifts and powers are received only upon the faithful development of the attributes of Christ in our personal lives as

122   Where Art Thou

well as obedient integration of the **rights of the priesthood**
into those attributes, or vice versa as the case may be.

POWERS OF HEAVEN		
(GIFTS GIVEN BY AN OMNIPOTENT FATHER TO RIGHTEOUS MEMBERS)		
INSPIRATION	M O R N I N G O F F I R S T R E S U R R E C T I O N	EXALTATIONS
PERSONAL REVELATION		THRONES
TESTIMONY		PRINCIPALITIES
JUDGMENT		POWERS
KNOWLEDGE		KINGDOMS
DISCERNMENT		GLORIES
WISDOM		DOMINIONS
HEALING		PATRIARCHAL PRIESTHOOD
VISIONS		BLESSINGS OF ABRAHAM, ISAAC AND JACOB
TONGUES		ETERNAL LIFE
PROPHECY		ALL HEIGHTS AND DEPTHS
MINISTERING ANGELS		CONTINUATION OF SEED
MIGHTY MIRACLES		KING AND QUEEN
LANGUAGES		
BEHOLDING OF ANGELS		
DIVERS KINDS OF TONGUES		

If we ask for these **powers of heaven** in virtue and holiness, we will be given them. We must, however, ask for them
as we need them and whenever we require them. It is for each
one of us to decide for our own selves which of these powers
we need, but the cardinal rule is that we must ask for them.

There is no injunction that is repeated more often in the
scriptures than: *"Ask, and ye shall receive . . ."* (see D&C 4:7).
Need we be afraid of asking in error? No! This is because as
we acquire the Christ—like attributes, we will be living so
much closer to the Savior that we will not be able to ask falsely.

Chapter 1   123

We will literally lose the desire to ask incorrectly.

In confirmation of this, we refer to two very meaningful scriptures, the first from Nephi, son of Lehi. *"Angels speak by the power of the Holy Ghost; wherefore, they speak the words of Christ. Wherefore, I said unto you, feast upon the words of Christ; for behold, **the words of Christ will tell you all things what ye should do"*** (see 2 Nephi 32:3). To feast upon the words of Christ is to be completely obedient to them.

Because Nephi (the son of Helaman) demonstrated such obedience, the Lord told him, *"And now, because thou has done this with such unwearyingness, behold, I will bless thee forever; and I will make thee mighty in word and in deed, in faith and in works; yea, even that all things shall be done unto thee according to thy word, **for thou shalt not ask that which is contrary to my will"*** (see Helaman 10:5).

In order to receive such great blessings for ourselves, we need the **powers of heaven** which are listed as gifts of the Holy Ghost. They include such ones as revelation, discernment, the power to heal, the power to be healed, wisdom, visions, and so on. There is probably no one who does not need such gifts. Perhaps the most needed and used is that of discernment — a gift that can enhance many situations and numerous circumstances. Think, for example, at how much we can use discernment as we seek to improve our perceptions.

Others of these **powers of heaven**, such as thrones, glories, dominions, and principalities (see D&C 132:19), will usually not be given to us until after our resurrection. It is very true that we will catch many glimpses of them. We may even see extended visions of them for specific purposes, but the fulness of them awaits our judgment from the Lord. It will be then that we will receive the complete realization and bestowal of all of these rewarding blessings. In fact, it will need to be in the morning of the first resurrection which, in and of itself, is a necessity for a Celestial Kingdom reward.

124   Where Art Thou

However, be sure that your vision is not on achieving a celestial glory. Remember the example of the professional football team used in Chapter Fourteen. Raise your sights sufficiently high so that you focus only on Exaltation in the Celestial Kingdom. These **powers of heaven** will only be bestowed upon those husbands and wives who are sealed by the Holy Spirit of Promise unto Exaltation (see D&C 131:1—4).

Our journey to that glorious destiny begins in this life with birth, followed by baptism and the gift of the Holy Ghost. At that point, our responsibility magnifies itself into a life of worthiness so that we can *qualify* for the **rights of the priesthood**, *develop* the **principles of righteousness**, and *earn* the **powers of heaven**. These can be categorized and listed, as we have done, but in reality they overlap and interact with each other.

We must be continually envisioning and working on the whole concept of our existence as well as on the component parts. Further, we must do it as families. Our vision of these three elements must be a funnel one. Tunnel vision of such teachings would be most useless, even deadly.

When we reach a high level of success in these three components as given in D&C 121:36, we will be ready to have our calling and election made sure. This subject will be covered in Chapter Fifteen.

One final thought is important even though it has been mentioned before. Your baptism was performed in the name of the Father and the Son and the Holy Ghost. Your temple sealings are likewise performed. The entry point (baptism) begins our eternal journey. The crowning ordinance (sealing) finalizes our reward for this journey, assuming, of course, that we have these made permanent by the Lord. From such a reward comes eternal, forever families.

Before we begin our journey, during it, and completing it, we will require constant interdependent interaction with each

Chapter 1   125

member of the Godhead. The stronger we construct that inter-dependency, the more sure we can be that we will receive and enjoy the **rights of the priesthood**, the **principles of righteousness**, and the **powers of heaven** in all of their fulness and glory.

This fulness and glory will prepare us to answer in the affirmative the four questions asked by Alma, the High Priest, to his people. The questions are as applicable to us today as they were then. *"Have ye walked, keeping yourselves blameless before God? Could you say, if you were called to die at this time, within yourselves, that ye have been sufficiently humble? That your garments have been cleansed and made white through the blood of Christ, who will come to redeem his people from their sins? Behold, are ye stripped of pride? I say unto you, if ye are not ye are not prepared to meet God. Behold ye must prepare quickly; for the kingdom of heaven is soon at hand, and such an one hath not eternal life"* (see Alma 5:27—28). To answer "Yes" to each of these four questions requires faithful and complete use of the priesthood as outlined in D&C 121:36.

126   Where Art Thou

Chapter Twelve

THE SPIRIT OF THE LORD IS GRIEVED

> **D&C 121:37** — *"That they [rights of the priesthood] may be conferred upon us, it is true; but when we undertake to cover our sins, or to gratify our pride, our vain ambition, or to exercise control or dominion or compulsion upon the souls of the children of men, in any degree of unrighteousness; behold, the heavens withdraw themselves; the Spirit of the Lord is grieved; and when it is withdrawn, Amen to the priesthood or authority of that man."*

Much has already been written about the rights of the priesthood but they are so critically important to our eternal progression that the Prophet Joseph Smith obviously felt an overpowering and oft—repeated need to instruct us as to their proper use in his writings. Even in this scripture, his language is very strong and forthright. He includes a warning as to what can happen to us if we abuse and misuse those priesthood rights. We must always be very careful that we use them in the Lord's prescribed way and in accordance with His outlined terms.

Why? Because it is not possible for any of us to obtain a knowledge of God without the full and correct use of the authority and powers of the priesthood. Learning obtained from secular sources, including the proverbial "school of hard knocks," will not reveal spiritual truths about God and His

128   Where Art Thou

mysteries. It is the Holy Priesthood that unlocks the door to
our Heavenly Father in order for Him to reveal to us the
teachings of the Savior and His Atonement, as well as what are
referred to as mysteries. Divine truths can only be learned and
understood through Divine Authority invested through the
rights of the priesthood to worthy men and women.

Please notice Joseph Smith's choice of words regarding
the misuse of those rights of the priesthood. He had translated
the Book of Mormon, and he knew its teachings very well.
How many times does this great book of scripture tell us that
the Nephites, when they were obedient and faithful, became
exceedingly righteous and true to the teachings of the prophets? During such periods, the people exercised the priesthood
with faith and purpose.

Then the oft—repeated cycle began. They could not hold
to that level of righteousness because pride, vain ambition,
unrighteous dominion, and compulsion crept in as inevitably
as the ocean tide comes in each day. As soon as any of these
evils entered their lives, the Nephites experienced a withdrawal
of the Holy Spirit and a loss of the priesthood. When the latter
occurs, rebaptism is necessary. Hence, the frequent mention
of this ordinance in the Book of Mormon.

The interesting fact is that the Nephites, when faithful,
were endowed with marvelous visions, wonderful spiritual
manifestations, forthright and strong prophets, and historic
recordings of great events. They were even blessed with
writings brought with them from Jerusalem so that their proud
heritage could remain in their minds. These were added to by
every prophet in their respective times. In addition, there were
many, many tremendous spiritual experiences that they en-
joyed but could not record. However, the abuse of the rights
of the priesthood resulted, inevitably, in the loss or withdrawal
of all of these blessings.

The sins mentioned in this scripture — pride, vain ambi-

Chapter 1   129

tion, unrighteous dominion, and compulsion — are frequently sins of comparison. People seem to have serious problems in avoiding comparing themselves with others. It happens to the best of people, and it occurs constantly, unless those individuals learn a very basic fact of life. It is such a **comparison that is a dead—end street** which leads nowhere fast.

For example, the Nephites witnessed the signs of the birth of Jesus in Jerusalem. These had been prophesied by Samuel the Lamanite. The Lord wanted them to know what these signs were so that the people could have no excuse. Included in the signs were a day, a night, and a day without the sun going down, and the appearance of a new star in the heavens.

Many of them knew the prophecies — those that would listen to the prophets. They knew the signs so well that they fell to the earth and became as if they were dead when the signs became recognizable. As a result, a large group repented of their sins. It is recorded in the Book of Mormon that, once they had accomplished this repentance, there were no contentions among them. Contentions are frequently brought on by, or have root in, such evils as pride, which, in turn, originates in unrighteous comparisons.

Despite such fascinating and tremendous experiences, it was only a few short years later that Satan gained possession of their hearts again. Disbelief, vain ambition, deceit, blindness to the truth, and pride crept into their lives. Why? Because comparison results in a "you've got more than me, so I'm going to get my share, even if it is at your expense" syndrome that manifests itself corruptly in people's lives.

The lesson is there in the Book of Mormon repeatedly: *"Now the cause of this iniquity of the people was this — Satan had great power, unto the stirring up of the people to do all manner of iniquity, and to the puffing them up with pride, tempting them to seek for power, and authority, and riches, and the vain things of the world."* (see 3 Nephi 6:15).

130   Where Art Thou

The interesting fact, in these oft—repeated situations, is that the Nephites did not turn to sin ignorantly. They knew the will of God concerning themselves. They had been taught thoroughly by great prophets who spoke strong, plain, and precious truths. Their rebellions against God were willful, deliberate, and knowing.

Therein lies one of the greatest sins that the Nephites, or anyone else for that matter, could commit. To willfully transgress against the Father, after having been taught and understanding the truth, always results in the greatest of punishments. The Holy Ghost is left with no choice but to withdraw; thus, the people are left to pay the penalties for their willful disobedience. God will not, and cannot, strive with individuals who constantly reject Him and kill His prophets, and who turn deliberately away from Him. Then, as stated in D&C 121:37, *"Amen to the priesthood, or the authority of that man* [people]."

Such negative behaviors are certainly not exclusive to the Book of Mormon days and peoples. According to modern day prophecies, we, ourselves, are now facing a season that will be like no other in the history of mankind. Satan has unleashed every evil scheme and plan and thought that he is capable of perpetuating. He is helping mankind experience a vast assortment of the most flagrant, decadent, and vilest perversions ever known to any generation.

Look, for example, at the ways in which many women are portrayed in television and movie shows. They are shown in the most degrading manner and situations even to the point where the lofty place granted to them by our Father has been crumbled and has been made most common. Even advertisements are produced in such a way as to sell many varieties of products depicting unnecessary nudity and degradation. Surely that which is most sacred becomes most common in the minds of men, boys, and children when it is portrayed so often in this manner.

The Lord named this as the Dispensation of the Fulness of

Chapter 1   131

Times. Lucifer is using it as the Dispensation for the Fulness of Evil. Unfortunately, well—meaning individuals are sitting idly by and allowing such depravity because supposedly there is a grey area between right and wrong, or white and black, and interference in such situations would deprive the participants of their "free agency." This is exactly what Satan wants us to think and feel. We are playing his game using his rules, and we frequently know that.

He is exceedingly clever. His battle plan does not include a frontal assault with a fully equipped army of his evil spirits. Rather, he is extremely subtle — a little lie there, a small compromise here, an overlooking of little sins, a rationalization of a principle here, and so on. An excellent example is the manner in which he uses the Freedom of Speech Amendment in the Bill of Rights. The result is clearly evident — more sexual perversion plainly out in the open for even small children to observe; greater use of the Lord's name taken in vain even by four— and five—year—olds; increased pursuit of highly questionable "leisure" activities, especially on the Sabbath Day; individuals manipulating illegal investment funds with little or no conscience; and a solid turning away from the Golden Rule and the Ten Commandments.

As we examine Satan's battle plan in detail, we find that Joseph Smith knew exactly what he was talking about. Central to that plan are such temptations as pride, vain ambition, unrighteous dominion, and compulsion. These are frequently stimulated by the mental syndrome that there is only so much wealth, time, products, food, and other worldly pursuits to go around. By comparison, there are so many people "out there" pursuing these relatively few riches, so why not grab yours first! While you are at it, grab as much as you can the first time, because you may not get a second chance; or if you do, the remains will not be worth having.

A good example of such a Satanistic—inspired way of thinking is the practice of birth control. Many nations have openly taught and even legislated such a practice. The motives have been to reduce the birth rates and to slow down the population growth patterns. Lucifer helps the people feel good about it because the hoped—for result is more for everyone who survives. His followers thrive on teaching that, without birth control, the world's food supply would soon be depleted, and we would all starve. They use "logical" arguments about production capabilities, moisture patterns, available productive soil, and human capacities to manufacture products without losing their leisure time rights or employment opportunities.

Even the faithful, who should know better, succumb to such arguments. The Lord, however, simply says *"For the earth is full, there is enough, and to spare . . ."* (see D&C 104:17). Those who are the most faithful know Him. They understand that He will inspire new sources, technologies, techniques, methods, and varieties in order to feed His children if they would but turn to Him and listen to His prophets.

What prevents us from doing that? The answer is basically the sin of comparison. It is a most common one amongst us. It tears at the basic fiber of one's soul. It can destroy individuals and nations so quickly and so easily. Yet it is a dead end street. The reason for all of this is that every one of our comparisons are totally unequal and unfair, although we would be the last to admit that such was the case.

You see, when we compare ourselves with others, we always use our own worst scenario and the other person's best one. It is as if we were dressed in our very worst clothes, and they are dressed in tuxedos or evening gowns which are Paris originals. You might just as well compare a mouse with an elephant for you would have just as much success.

We use our worst because we can then feel justified in our pride and vain ambitions. No one should have more than we do. No one should feel better about what they have and are than we should feel. No one should outplay or out—perform

Chapter 1   133

us. All of these examples, and many others, are the reasonings of Lucifer. He wants you to feel negative and put down. He does not have to do it to you. You will do it for yourself. When you do, you will commit more and greater sins. Then, you are in his power.

Two of the ingredients in comparison are pride and ambition. Most of us do not want anyone to win over us for then we would be the losers. Who wants to be a loser? We all want to be the winners. That is why some athletic coaches perpetuate, and imbue in players the philosophy that winning is the only thing — even if we have to win at all costs.

Sadly enough, to win at any cost stimulates us to live how and for what others expect of us, or from us. But the more we base our lives on the expectations of others, the more insecure and pretentious we become. This is because we are seeking for our victories in public while, at the same time, we are suffering private defeats in our morals, values, and Christ—like attributes. Stephen R. Covey states that *"we do not have lasting public victories until we have successful private ones."*

Was not the pattern for this set by the Savior when He went into the wilderness for forty days and forty nights to win His private battle with Himself? Was He not then able to withstand the immediate three direct assaults upon Him by the evil Lucifer? Even though weak in body, He was so strong in spirit because He had won His private battle first. How many times have you heard — first the thought, and then the deed?

Comparisons breed insecurities. Insecure people generally borrow strength from the authority, title, position, or experience of another person who has assumed some significance in their lives. For example, a young man may tell his sister that, "Dad said you were to do . . ." Usually he knows very well that she would not even consider it if she thought that the instruction was coming from him instead of the father. Instead of relaying the messages and making decisions on our own, we frequently use compulsion or unrighteous dominion.

134   Where Art Thou

"You had better do it, or I'll tell Dad," is a common illustration.

Comparison is a weapon used and encouraged by Satan. He wants us to feel superior or inferior to others. " . . .*Stand by thyself, come not near to me, for I am holier than thou . . .* " (see Isaiah 65:5). Such attitudes are cancerous. They are self—defeating, infectious, and contagious. They destroy beautiful feelings of love, charity, and wisdom as well as all other Christ—like attributes. As written, *"Only by pride cometh contention: but with the well advised is wisdom"* (see Proverbs 13:10). To feel superior is to be prideful or to exercise unrighteous dominion. To feel inferior is to deny the Divine parentage that we have or to punish ourselves needlessly.

As surely as the sun rises each morning, contention draws us further away from the Savior because our thoughts are not centered on Him but on selfish pursuits. We forget about Him even though our conscience keeps gnawing at us. We fail to thank Him because we are accomplishing our desires without Him. *"Ye do not remember the Lord your God in the things with which he hath blessed you, but ye do always remember your riches, not to thank the Lord your God for them; yea, your hearts are not drawn out unto the Lord, but they do swell with great pride, unto boasting and unto great swelling, envyings, strifes, malice, persecutions, and murders, and all manner of iniquities"* (see Helaman 13:22).

On the other hand, the absence of comparison in our lives promotes our sense of worth, identity, self—esteem, and humility. We become filled with love because we learn to value differences in others, not compete against them. We learn how to adapt to those differences in others, rather to be envious of them. We learn how to praise without twinges of jealousy, to express gratitude without becoming ambitious, and to honor others without the loss of our own dignity.

We become true disciples of the living Jesus Christ if we can reach and maintain that stage in our lives when even

Chapter 1   135

sincere praises for outward acts almost embarrasses us instead of inflating our egos. We seek purity from God for our efforts in His Kingdom rather than praise or rewards from other human beings. We are accomplishing what we have already promised by covenant to do; thus, we are building integrity within ourselves and with the Father.

Even when chastened, we should not lose our perspective because chastenings appropriately and correctly applied ultimately work for our improvement, if we have the right attitude. *"Now no chastening for the present seemeth to be joyous, but grievous: nevertheless afterward it yieldeth the peaceable fruit of righteousness unto them which are exercised thereby"* (see Hebrews 12:11).

In order to avoid participating in the Dispensation for the Fulness of Evil, we must find safety. It will not be provided by governments or economic wealth and position, or in pleasure—seeking activities. These will all fail. Just being a member of the Church will not be a guarantee. In fact, if we misuse or neglect the rights of the priesthood, it will be better that we had not been born. *"But whoso breaketh this covenant after he hath received it, and altogether turneth therefrom, shall not have forgiveness in this world nor in the world to come."* (see D&C 84:41).

The only real places of refuge will be the temples of the Lord and in the sanctity of a righteous, dedicated home. There we will find peace, safety, light, and sacred havens. There are numerous unseen sentinels watching over and guarding the temples. Angels attend every door and every session, and we must pass by them. The responsibility for keeping our homes sacred, and for those residing within to be worthy at all times, rests on our shoulders. If we have dedicated our homes properly, angels will also watch over and protect them as well as the faithful inhabitants.

An important part of the temple includes our protective garments and covenants. These fill us with a faith that is as a

136   Where Art Thou

living fire. The strength of that flame will enable us to hold to
the rod and to taste of the sweetest fruits of the truths in the
Gospel. These are the covenants included in the rights of the
priesthood as discussed in Chapter Eleven. These covenants
are found no where else.

Thus, we come back to the warning of the Prophet Joseph
Smith that to properly exercise those rights, and to be worthy at
all times to enter the temple, we must avoid pride, vain ambition,
unrighteous dominion, and compulsion, as well as any other
degree of transgressive action. If we avoid or overcome these
problems, we will be worthy to find haven in the temple when we
are called at any time and under any circumstance, particularly at
the time when the Savior returns again for His Second Coming.

The problems listed in the Prophet's warning are frequently
caused by our having too short a perspective on life's real
purpose, or having a hazy idea of our ultimate goal, or both. These
are the same problems that we experience in overcoming the
natural man spoken of by King Benjamin in Mosiah, Chapter 3.
To truly value the rights of the priesthood, and to change the
natural man into a spiritual one, we must develop a much longer
and truer perspective of our ultimate goal of Exaltation. Then, we
must have a well—constructed, definitive plan of action, the
pursuit of which will avoid the previously stated problems.

A few suggestions are offered for your consideration.
These are those which will help you extend your vision in
order to sharply focus on your ultimate goal. The concept is for
you to work backwards from that clearly defined goal. This is
done through the use of well—thought out and planned
intermediate steps. If you forget the final goal and place all
your attention on the intermediate steps, these become problem situations or stumbling blocks. By working backwards,
the intermediate steps constitute stepping stones.

*Think seriously about tomorrow. You can only reap
what you sow. Planning ahead will help you avoid many

Chapter 1   137

disappointments as well as make any adjustments that will be needed to minimize last minute problems or failures.

*Be willing to use your imagination. Enlarge your vision by always including your Heavenly Father in your plans. Paul stated, *"If God be for us, who can stand against us?"* (see JST Romans 8:31) You always do far better when you establish a creative, interdependent relationship with Father.

*Strive consistently for quality obedience and sacrifice in your life. There will definitely come a time when you will be required to report on your earthly stewardship to the Lord. An important part of that report includes your use of the rights of the priesthood. It will also include a report on the levels of obedience and sacrifice that you have achieved in your life. It would therefore be wise to achieve and maintain the highest level of quality in these laws as soon as you possibly can.

*Have fortitude. Set your course directly for Exaltation and develop a very clear vision of what that means. Never waiver from your course. Avoid confusing the goal with the processes you must use in order to achieve it. The goal is Exaltation in the Celestial Kingdom — nothing less. The processes include baptism, the Holy Ghost, justification, the Holy Priesthood, sanctification, making your calling and election sure, and ultimate perfection.

*Enjoy what you are doing. The world's idea of fun and pleasure too often includes or creates satire, putdowns, sarcasm, humor at another's expense, pride, compulsion, comparisons, and spiteful retaliation. When the Father cast Lucifer out of the Garden of Eden, He said, "...I will put enmity between thee and the woman, between thy seed and her seed; and he shall bruise thy head, and thou shalt bruise his heel" (see Moses 4:21). Enmity is hatred and/or opposition. To love the Savior is to "hate" His opposition. If we build spiritual enjoyment in our service to God, we will turn against evil in all of its forms and at all times.

138   Where Art Thou

*Develop congruence in your life. Incongruence between your values and your experiences develops conflicting emotions. Learning to love and trust those around you will reduce those conflicts. Incongruence between your own self—worth and your daily experiences causes stress, anxieties, illnesses, and low self—esteem. Train yourself to avoid thinking about how others view you, and you will rapidly increase your personal self—worth. This, in turn, will then stimulate thoughts for self—improvement, which, when acted upon, gives you the satisfaction of feeling that you are in charge of your life — a requirement for internal peace and increased congruence.

In Proverbs we read, *"He that covereth his sins shall not prosper: but whoso confesseth and forsaketh them shall have mercy"* (see Proverbs 28:13). We live in a constantly changing world of experiences. We react to those experiences in accordance with our perceptions. Those reactions result in our behavior which is the goal—directed attempt to satisfy our basic needs, which, in turn, arise out of our perceptions. The question that each of us must answer is: "Will those needs be the most spiritual ones that are in our power to create?"

The Prophet Joseph Smith realized that we needed to find and use an anchor in this constantly changing world of experiences. This anchor includes the rights of the priesthood as a critical component. *"Beloved, now we are the sons of God. and it doth not yet appear what we shall be: but we know that, when he shall appear, we shall be like him; for we shall see him as he is. And every man that hath this hope in him purifieth himself, even as he is pure"* (see 1 John 3:2—3).

When we lock on to an anchor based on such beautiful components, we will strive always to satisfy our needs in highly spiritual ways because our perceptions will also be highly spiritual. If we play games with the rights of the priesthood, we will always have severe problems with pride, vain ambitions, and varying degrees of unrighteousness. In this case, the converse is also true. When we honor, and are

Chapter 1   139

obedient to, the rights of the priesthood, we will be faithful, righteous, and virtuous.

Then, and only then, will we be in the condition spoken of by Jesus when He taught His disciples: *"Then saith Jesus unto his disciples, If any man will come after me, let him deny himself, and take up his cross, and follow me. And now for a man to take up his cross, is to deny himself all ungodliness, and every worldly lust, and keep my commandments"* (see JST Matthew 16:24).

Where Art Thou

Chapter Thirteen

CHRIST-LIKE ATTRIBUTES

D&C 121:41—42 — *"No power or influence can or ought to be maintained by virtue of the priesthood, only by persuasion, by long—suffering, by gentleness and meekness, and by love unfeigned; by kindness, and pure knowledge, which shall greatly enlarge the soul without hypocrisy, and without guile."*

There is no question that the personal attributes given in these two verses are specifically important to each of us if we are to avoid unrighteous use of the priesthood. The implications are very powerful. We should have no doubt that if we are to avoid such pitfalls, and righteously use the priesthood, we must be long—suffering, gentle, meek, loving, and knowledgeable.

To further understand these implications, we need to review two very important scriptures. Peter tells us that, *"Whereby are given unto us exceeding great and precious promises: that by these ye might be partakers of the divine nature, having escaped the corruption that is in the world through lust. And besides this, giving all **diligence,** add to your faith **virtue;** and to virtue **knowledge;** And to knowledge **temperance;** and to temperance **patience;** and to patience **godliness;** and to godliness **brotherly kindness;** and to brotherly kindness **charity"** (see 2 Peter 1:4—7).

142   Where Art Thou

The Lord revealed to Joseph Smith similar instruction, *"And **faith, hope, charity and love,** with an eye single to the glory of God, qualify him for the work. Remember **faith, virtue, knowledge, temperance, patience, brotherly kindness, godliness, charity, humility, diligence"** (see D&C 4:5—6). It would appear, therefore, that we must acquire as many Christ—like attributes as possible if we are to apply the principles of righteousness in our lives as discussed in Chapter Eleven, pages 117—120. We cannot possibly use the priesthood without developing such attributes.

In speaking to His newly called disciples, Jesus gave them a number of instructions including the injunction, *"The disciple is not above his master: but everyone that is perfect shall be as his master"* (see Luke 6:40). The Savior was teaching us that we must ever be aware of our imperfections, and that we must always remember that when we see a mote or fault in another person, we usually manage to forget the beam or fault in ourselves. He also was letting us know that we cannot exercise His priesthood, except as He does.

In that same scripture, our Master clearly stated that everyone can be as perfect as Himself. He gave us the pattern that we must follow — by growing from grace to grace as He did. *"And Jesus increased in wisdom and stature and in favour with God and man"* (see Luke 2:52). Our growth must be from Christ—like attribute to Christ—like attribute using the ten—step process to sanctification as outlined in Chapter Three, page 32. The Lord has given us a complete assurance that we can become perfect by following these instructions.

There should be no question of "if." The "how" we can become perfect is through sanctification, provided we are willing to pay the price. Once that commitment is made, the only remaining decision is "when" we will actually get started on the process or journey. Otherwise, we must remain filthy still, unable to use the priesthood in righteousness; and even if a church leader does not restrict us in that use, our own sense of right and wrong will.

Chapter 1   143

To encourage you in that decision, the following concepts are provided for your review or consideration. They are worthy of serious examination.

"Yea, come unto Christ, and be perfected in him, and deny yourselves of all ungodliness; and if ye shall deny yourselves of all ungodliness, and love God with all your might, mind, and strength, then is his grace sufficient for you, that by his grace ye may be perfect in Christ; and if by the grace of God ye are perfect in Christ, ye can in nowise deny the power of God" (see Moroni 10:32).

*A study of the scriptures already cited should impress us deeply with the need we have to come unto Christ. The prophets have certainly not hidden this instruction from us. But, to come unto Christ requires action on our part. It demands much more from us than mere verbal expressions. It solidly places upon us the necessity to acquire Christ—like attributes; else how could we come unto Christ? We already know that unclean and unworthy individuals cannot be in His presence.

*The Master's personality reflects the attributes listed in 2 Peter 1:4—7 and D&C 4:5—6. Too often, people ascribe to the Savior a generalized goodness or an abstract virtuousness. However, the attributes He prescribes are far more specific and identifiable. If we are to become like Him, we must be genuinely active in developing these same detailed qualities in our own lives. This is the only way we can demonstrate that we are not above the Master and that we are using His priesthood virtuously.

*When we ponder deeply on these Christ—like attributes, the impressive fact emerges that the capacity to love is at the very center of all of our obedience to God's commandments. It was the Lord who stated that, " . . .*Thou shalt love the Lord thy God with all thy heart, and with all thy soul, and with all thy mind. This is the first and great commandment. And the second is like unto it, Thou shalt love thy neighbor as thyself.* **On these two commandments hang all the law and the**

144   Where Art Thou

prophets" (see Matthew 22:37—40).

*The Lord's anger and indignation is properly kindled against us when we refuse to be fully obedient to these two great commandments, which tell us unequivocally to become like Him. Despite our knowing of His anger, we often find ourselves speaking publicly of our love for the Savior, but doing the opposite in other situations, including denying Him as Peter did when the cock crowed three times. When we are thus hypocritical, we make a hollow mockery out of our professions of love for Him who died for us.

*If we lack Christ—like attributes in our lives, we inflict so much misery upon ourselves as well as upon others, including our loved ones. This misery publicly indicates that we are walking the path laid out by Lucifer instead of the one prescribed by the Lord. *"Wherefore, men are free according to the flesh; and all things are given unto them which are expedient unto man. And they are free to choose liberty and eternal life, through the great Mediator of all men, or to choose captivity and death, for he seeketh that all men might be miserable like unto himself according to the captivity and power of the devil"* (see 2 Nephi 2:27). Many times a person is heard to say that he or she is only hurting themselves in committing so—called little sins. Nothing could be further from the truth, because the reality is that we deny our righteous association with others, even in the little sins.

*In the pre-existence, we very definitely made the decision not to follow Satan. We wanted no part of his misery. We must now be determined never to renege on that decision in this phase of our existence. The surest way to avoid going backwards is to move steadily forward in the acquisition of these Christ—like attributes. The more we become like Christ, the less influence Satan can have on us. Remember, we can never stand still. If we are not moving forward, we surely will be going backwards. There is no neutral ground in this work of the Father.

Chapter 1   145

*When what Jesus is begins to develop and flourish more fully in us, we will be filled with awe and godliness. When we come unto Christ in character and in deeds, we truly become His sons and daughters. When what we are parallels the great example of the Savior, we can totally respond to His beautifully simple, and simply beautiful, invitation to *"Come, follow me!"* It will then follow that we will be able to feel His loving arms around us whenever we genuinely need to have that experience.

*"*And he said unto the children of men: Follow thou me. Wherefore, my beloved brethren, can we follow Jesus save we shall be willing to keep the commandments of the Father?"* (see 2 Nephi 31:10). Just as Jesus served His apprenticeship, so must we serve ours if we desire to be justified and sanctified in Him. *"Then answered Jesus and said unto them: Verily, verily, I say unto you, the Son of Man can do nothing of himself, but what he seeth the Father do: for what things soever he doeth, these also doeth the Son likewise"* (see John 5:19). We can only speculate what Jesus really meant by this scripture. That is not wise; but the fact remains that what He has done is a divine part and repetition of an eternal plan that precedes Christ Himself.

*Just as the Father and the Son were completely united in all things, so must we be united in Christ by acquiring all of the Christ—like attributes. Inasmuch as our characters consist of those distinctive qualities on which our actions are based, and which set us apart from others as well as from each other, it automatically follows that to have a Christ—like character, we must possess Christ—like attributes. *"And now, behold, my beloved brethren, this is the way; and **there is none other way nor name given under heaven whereby man can be saved in the kingdom of God.** And now, behold, this is the doctrine of Christ, and the only and true doctrine of the Father, and of the Son, and of the Holy Ghost, which is one God, without end . . ."* (see 2 Nephi 31:21). The type of salvation referred to here by the Savior is not just to be raised from the dead. It means Exaltation, and nothing less.

ATTRIBUTE NUMBER 1:

FAITH: WHAT IS IT?

It is significant to note that the Lord mentions the attribute of **faith** twice in D&C 4. There are only two attributes so repeated — the other being charity. Perhaps the Lord's emphasis on this quality is necessary because it is the one Christ—like attribute which weakens first when trials and adversities enter our lives. Since it is the first to weaken, we ought to make it twice as strong as we otherwise might. Hence, the need for the Lord to say it twice. Repetition always serves to give added importance.

Faith is the fundamental principle of life which draws our spirits into communion with a power greater than our own. History is full of examples of individuals, communities, tribes, and nations reaching out to a power greater than themselves. The reality of life is that people frequently knew not the true and living God, so anything became acceptable as a substitute — golden calves, animals, birds, totem poles, to mention just a few.

Our **faith** must be centered in and interdependent with the Godhead. As we commune with them, we do so through the power of the Holy Ghost whose mission includes bringing all things to our remembrance, to show us things as they are and as they are to come, and to teach us about the Godhead, while, at the same time, witnessing to the divinity of the Savior.

Men often try to substitute reason for **faith**, but reason is not an accurate source nor is it a reliable guide in searching for all truth. Reason rests on the concept that man can solve or understand all of life's truths; yet much truth rests upon unproven evidences and perceptions. If these are false or based upon insufficient data, the "truth" will be highly suspect. Reason also is used to rationalize our desires as constituting what is best for us. When these are not fulfilled, we

Chapter 1   147

waiver in our commitment and testimony. It is hard for us to remain very strong in our **faith**, when we do not get our way as determined by our selfish reasonings.

Inborn in every person is a strong instinct to worship something or someone. Perhaps this is a result of being born with the Light of Christ within us. Regardless, it is true that most people look upward to heaven in searching for a power greater that their own. This looking upward is an expression of **faith**. As a member of the Church, your **faith** in our Heavenly Father should give you an understanding of what is happening to you today, as well as why it is taking place. In addition, it should provide for you a vision and an optimism for your own personal future and that of those over whom you exercise righteous dominion.

Faith is complete reliance on God the Father and His Son Jesus Christ. You can have such reliance because of the certainty that God is a God of truth and cannot lie (see Ether 3:12). This means that He will never ever lead you astray, even to the smallest degree. He will never permit His earthly prophets and other priesthood leaders to deliberately lead you astray either. Only the Godhead, however, is uniquely qualified to provide hope, confidence, and strength sufficient to help us to overcome the world, and to help us rise above our own human failings of the natural man.

Faith is also the power to do anything and everything that we have righteously covenanted to do. *"And Christ hath said: If ye will have faith in me ye shall have power to do whatsoever thing is expedient in me"* (see Moroni 7:33). Our **faith** is manifested in our actions, and, after we recognize the good we have done, our **faith** increases until it changes into the knowledge that we can repeatedly do those same good things with the same good results. In turn, our knowledge increases our **faith.**

Given all of the above, **faith** is the great governing principle which provides us with power, dominion, and authority

148   Where Art Thou

over all spiritual and temporal things. Witness, for example, Peter's attempt to walk on the water towards his Savior. It helps us to understand how all things exist as well as what we must do to become agreeable to the will of God.

FAITH: HOW TO ACQUIRE IT:

The acquisition of **faith** in the Godhead and in oneself is the responsibility of every living soul who desires to know the truth of all things pertaining to this life and the eternal life to come. With such a great responsibility on our shoulders, how do we acquire an unlimited **faith**?

*Trust in Jesus Christ and in His power to bless you with all things which shall be for your good. Let Him be your tutor without placing conditions or qualifications upon His will concerning you personally.

*Apply all of the Gospel teachings and temple covenants in your life. Avoid being selective as if you were attending a "smorgasborg" from which you could choose according to your likes. Be as totally submersed spiritually in the Gospel as you were physically in the waters of baptism.

*Pray with a sincere heart and with real intent, seeking not for signs, but for evidences and manifestations of the truth of that which you are doing, thinking, and studying.

*Become interdependent with the Godhead rather than placing your belief in people. *"Set your affection on things above, not on things on the earth"* (see Colossians 3:2). The possibility exists that some people will disappoint, even anger you, but the Lord will *never* let you down.

*Consecrate yourself to the work of the Savior rather that to your own selfish needs and comforts. Once you determine to center your life on Christ, all other values become crystal clear and correctly prioritized.

Chapter 1   149

*Be singleminded in focusing on the purposes of the Godhead even though you do not fully or even partially understand them.

*Do not procrastinate the day of your repentance (see Helaman 15:7). Begin your journey towards complete justification without any detours or delays.

*Feast upon the words of Christ in the scriptures and on the teachings of the prophets. Avoid just reading or glancing at them. Ponder them deeply. To feast upon the words of Christ is to press forward and to endure to the end (see 2 Nephi 31:20).

*Yield complete obedience in all things to the Lord and His commandments, The result will be soul—satisfying security and peace in your mind and heart.

*Hunger and thirst after righteousness so that you will always be clean and pure enough to enjoy the full and constant companionship of the Holy Ghost.

*Move beyond just a willingness to help others into the deepest meanings of the principle of charity.

*Remember that you will never be tempted beyond your capacity to endure. You will be stretched as far as possible in your tests, but you will never be broken. Such extensive testing is necessary for you to become as refined as pure gold. You will endure a "Zion's Camp" sometime in your life.

*Control Satan's influence in your life by keeping him out of your daily activities. Never give him even the slightest foothold in your actions or thoughts. If you do, then accept the responsibility and repent immediately. Reference is often made to the portrait of the Savior standing at the front door and knocking — waiting for your invitation to enter your life. You can rest assured that Satan is likewise standing at the back door waiting for a similar invitation from you.

150   Where Art Thou

*Examine with microscopic care your reasons for living the Gospel. Be sure that your motives are clean and pure (see Alma 32:13—14). Once solid commitments are made in your mind, physical actions are far more successful.

*Express your testimony daily. The more you repeat it, the stronger your **faith** will become. Each expression of your testimony weaves one more strand in the cable of your **faith.**

ATTRIBUTE NUMBER 2:

VIRTUE: WHAT IS IT?

The Savior's injunction is to " . . .*let **virtue** garnish thy thoughts unceasingly; then shall thy confidence wax strong in the presence of God; . . .*" (see D&C 121:45). President Spencer W. Kimball always espoused, *"First the thought, then the deed,"*

The Christ—like attribute of **virtue** includes personal chastity (complete abstinence from *all* moral relationships and experiences except with your lawful husband or wife); clean thoughts (constantly replacing evil ones with good ones); and personal integrity (always being completely faithful to your promises and commitments).

This attribute of **virtue** also consists of sincerity (having no selfish or hidden agenda purposes in your heart or actions); purity (becoming more and more sanctified each day); and simplicity (possessing no desire to use or take advantage of anyone for your personal gain or honor).

Virtue means to be willing to sacrifice your own life rather than to give up your values or to deny Christ: *"He who seeketh to save his life shall lose it; and he that loseth his life for my sake shall find it"* (see JST Matthew 10:39). To seek to save your life for the wrong reasons is to sacrifice your values. To lose your life for the sake of Jesus is to have the Holy Ghost constantly guiding your every thought and deed;

Chapter 1   151

to be steadfastly holding to the moral and spiritual highway or rod by developing your spiritual self at the expense of your natural self; and to use the powers of God [the priesthood] righteously.

VIRTUE; HOW TO ACQUIRE IT:

"We call no man virtuous till he has passed from innocence to the conquest of temptation. It takes a wise man to be virtuous" (David Starr Jordan). To acquire **virtue** in our lives is to become pure in heart and mind, thus achieving an increasingly higher level of thought—control. This, in turn, leads to being justified, sanctified, and exalted.

Elder Dallin H. Oaks has given us four keys whereby this high level of thought—control can be developed. (see *Pure in Heart*, pp. 140—151).

*Alter our attitudes and priorities by admitting our own imperfections regardless of whether they are inherited or environmental. Honestly assess our weaknesses, accept them as our own, strip away the defenses we have accumulated to protect our innermost feelings from hurt and pain, then make the necessary changes.

*Purify our thoughts by *instantly* substituting a good thought for a bad one as soon as you think it. Good thoughts can be found in the scriptures, hymns, writings, poems, and other wholesome places. Complete purity of thought is possible to attain using this technique; but, remember that it takes one good thought to replace each bad one. There are no shortcuts in this process (see Chapter Ten, pp. 106—108).

*Reform our motives and be as concerned about our sins of omission as we are about our sins of commission. A sin of omission is an act that we have left undone because of being lazy, passive, or irresponsible.

*Perfect our desires by deliberately altering our feelings

when they are unrighteous, immoral, or impure. This is done in the same way as changing our thoughts.

ATTRIBUTE NUMBER 3:

KNOWLEDGE: WHAT IS IT?

Knowledge is the acquisition of information through study, pondering, and experiencing — personal and vicarious. All information gives us power to act, to speak, or to become; but all information is not of equal value. Thus, when Jesus asked, "...*What think ye of Christ?...*" (see Matthew 22:42), He was asking us to search out our most vunerable thoughts.

God has blessed us with intelligence which is light and truth. This permits us to sift through the information we acquire and to discard that which is of no value or which is wrong. No—value information is most often based on misperceptions or gossip. That is why intelligence is the wise use of **knowledge.**

The **knowledge** which is of greatest value to us consists of understanding the personality and attributes of the Godhead and our individual role in their plan (see Chapter Four, pages 37—41). There is no limit to the acquisition of this type of knowledge because, as we apply it in our lives, our understanding continually expands. That is why the GLORY OF GOD IS INTELLIGENCE.

We should remember, however, that it is not the acquisition of **knowledge** which challenges our faith. Rather, it is the danger of thinking that we have learned enough. Small minds are filled with such conceit. True education is not measured in secular terms of honors, degrees, titles, or positions. It is acquired by constantly comparing your studies and learnings to your God—like character, then discarding that which would diminish that character. True believers attend church meetings and temple experiences with the purpose in mind of

Chapter 1 153

adding at least one new understanding to that balance in their God—like characters.

Having wisdom gives us courage to accomplish these actions because we understand that the wise course of action is not always the popular one. You must not try to change the truth to fit into man's explanations. *"Truth must be repeated over and over again because error is constantly being preached round about"* (Goethe).

KNOWLEDGE: HOW TO ACQUIRE IT

We need to be literally thirsty for **knowledge.** The Prophet Joseph Smith taught that we can be saved no faster that we gain a **knowledge** of the Gospel, including developing our interdependent relationships with the Godhead. Nephi wrote, " . . .*Wherefore, I said unto you, feast upon the words of Christ; for behold, the words of Christ will tell you all things what ye should do"* (see 2 Nephi 32:3).

Here are a few specific suggestions on how we can feast upon the words of Christ and His Prophets in order to gain **knowledge.**

*Study what you read. This requires you to think as you read and it develops more accurate relationships with what you have already learned. It corrects some incorrect perceptions.

*Memorize selected scriptures. This gives you a sense of mastery of self which is a very important ingredient in self—esteem and self—assurance as well as in personal confidence.

*Pray before and after you study to increase inspiration, understanding, and retention, as well as to evidence your humility before God.

*Take time to meditate and ponder on what you have studied. This stretches your power to understand and to associate prior learnings.

154   Where Art Thou

*Sift truth from error by constantly listening to the Holy Ghost. Just because a great person writes or says something, it does not automatically mean that it is true.

*Keep your mind from being a dumping ground for other people's garbage, including their gossip and sick humor.

*Seek for truths beyond your ability to reason. These truths are referred to as *"hidden treasures"* (see D&C 89:19). They must, however, be based on what you have already learned to be true. Be an inquisitive learner but only for truth. Avoid putting your capabilities down. They are usually greater than you think.

*Practice what you learn. George Washington stated, *"Truth will ultimately prevail when there are pains taken to bring it to light."* This must be through your actions (see John 7:17).

*Use the scriptures, temple ordinances, and writings of the Prophets as your measuring rods for determining what is true. When conflicts arise, stay with the rods.

*Search for **knowledge** in holy places. Stay away from those unrighteous dissenters who teach without the Spirit.

*Understand that belief, faith, and **knowledge** are not synonymous. Alma gave us strong comprehension of this: *"Now I ask is this faith? Behold, I say unto you, Nay; for if a man knoweth a thing he hath no cause to believe, for he knoweth it. And now as I said concerning faith — faith is not to have a perfect **knowledge** of things; therefore, if ye have faith ye hope for things which are not seen, which are true"* (see Alma 32:18,21). Our task is to acquire a **perfect knowledge** of all things.

ATTRIBUTE NUMBER 4:

TEMPERANCE: WHAT IS IT?

Historically, **temperance** has most frequently been used

Chapter 1   155

to demonstrate abstinence from alcoholic beverages. The Gospel definition for this attribute centers on moderation, self—restraint, and abstinence. However, it extends far beyond what we eat or drink. For example: *"a man who cannot control his temper is not likely to control his passion, and no matter what his pretensions in religion, he moves in daily life very close to the animal plane"* (President David O. McKay).

Temperance is the close associate of patience and tolerance. It should be the real motive for why we exercise self—control. It is the critical attribute that we need to postpone many of our "natural" feelings and to bridle many of our passions. In the process of such postponement, we become much less critical of others.

Temperance means that we are completely able to control our emotions — to be the master of our feelings and to put the "spiritual" man in charge of our words, deeds, and feelings. *"Be ye angry, and not sin; let not the sun go down on your wrath"* (see Ephesians 4:26). Ingersoll penned: *"Anger blows out the lamp of the mind."*

TEMPERANCE: HOW TO ACQUIRE IT

In acquiring **temperance**, Alma gave us some sage advice: *"And now, as ye have begun to teach the word even so I would that ye should continue to teach; and I would that ye would be diligent and temperate in all things. See that ye are not lifted up unto pride; yea, see that ye do not boast in your own wisdom, nor of your much strength. Use boldness, but not overbearance; and also see that ye bridle all your passions, that ye may be filled with love; see that ye refrain from idleness"* (see Alma 38:10—12).

Alma's advice is excellent. Here are a few practical suggestions for implementing it, if you choose to do so.

*Think before you react. Remember your emotions are

156   Where Art Thou

based on your perceptions. If they are wrong, your reactions will be incorrect. Take time to check out your perceptions.

*Master your emotions before reacting and usually over—reacting. Postpone your reply, walk away, count to one hundred, have a prayer, then respond. Another technique is to ask "find out" questions in order to acquire all of the facts, then react.

*Do not over—indulge in anything. Use moderation in all things (see D&C 89:18—21).

*Be tolerant of other people's mistakes and weaknesses. Snap judgments are frequently based upon inadequate data.

*Find good reasons to praise others. Proactively train yourself to be positive. This means to make good things happen in your life.

*Control your temper. Anger is one of Satan's most commonly used weapons. He is very willing to help you do irreparable damage to others. Once spoken in haste, angry words can never be recalled.

ATTRIBUTE NUMBER 5:

PATIENCE: WHAT IS IT?

In its most simplistic definition, **patience** is learning to wait for what you want. To do so, you need endurance. *"But if we hope for that we see not, then do we with **patience** wait for it"* (see Romans 8:25).

Church history is replete with good examples of the **patience** exhibited by the early pioneers who endured pains, trials, deaths, and persecutions without complaint about the supposed unfairness of a loving God. Church prophecies inform us that many similar, even worse, experiences await us to test our faith and **patience.**

Chapter 1   157

This attribute is another form of self—control like unto temperance. It involves an exercise of forbearance under provocation as illustrated in the Christ—like principle of "... *whosoever shall smite thee on the right cheek, turn to him the other also"* (see Matthew 5:39).

Patience is composure under stress. "...*Continue in patience until ye are perfected"* (see D&C 67:13). It is understanding the faults of another when all is not going smoothly. The Lord understood this when He commanded us to do good to those that hate us or spitefully use us, and to forgive those who curse us or persecute us (see Matthew 5:38).

PATIENCE: HOW TO ACQUIRE IT

It is entirely possible that the attribute of **patience** will prove to be one of the hardest to acquire. The Lord obviously was not overlooking its importance when He said, *"And seek the face of the Lord always, that in patience ye may possess your souls, and ye shall have eternal life"* (see D&C 101:38).

*Avoid tempestuous behavior that you will regret later. Train yourself to assess the consequences of your actions before you carry them out. Use a good evaluative technique to help in that assessment, including some trusted friend if you cannot be objective about yourself.

*Consider the Lord's policy of proving us first and rewarding us later. Many future rewards will require your **patience** and endurance even though you are earning those rewards as you live.

*Dovetail **patience** into love. You can endure much better and much more if you love patiently.

*Develop self—control. Instant gratification results in few long range rewards. Sometimes you have to step back from the forest in order to re—find the path through it.

158 Where Art Thou

*Yield your soul to Christ and center your life in Him. *"In your **patience** possess ye your souls"* (see Luke 21:19).

*Study the many examples of people who exhibit great **patience** in tribulations. When your own is being tested, bear your testimony. There is a strong relationship between **patience** and testimony.

ATTRIBUTE NUMBER 6:

BROTHERLY KINDNESS: WHAT IS IT?

Kindness always involves at least one other person. It is the manifestation of a sincere interest in someone else accompanied by a desire to help by being gracious, benevolent, sympathetic, and tender. *"And be ye kind one to another, tenderhearted, forgiving one another, even as God for Christ's sake hath forgiven you"* (see Ephesians 4:32).

Brotherly kindness involves a willingness to avoid tearing down, reviling, or persecuting others. This includes making fun of, using sarcasm against, or speaking put—downs to others. *"And the King shall answer and say unto them, Verily I say unto you, Inasmuch as ye have done it unto one of the least of these my brethren, ye have done it unto me"* (see Matthew 25:40).

This counsel from the Lord applies equally to positive situations as well as negative ones. You have done it unto the Lord whether you praise or put—down someone. In developing the Christ—like attribute of **brotherly kindness**, our relationship with others should be positive and loving.

BROTHERLY KINDNESS: HOW TO ACQUIRE IT

The governing principle in all of our dealings with others was given to us by the Savior: *"Therefore, all things whatsoever ye would that men should do to you, do ye even so to*

Chapter 1   159

them; for this is the law and the prophets" (see Matthew 7:12; 3 Nephi 14:12).

*Be loyal to one another, especially family members and leaders. Avoid backbiting. If you disagree, discuss it face—to—face; be willing to compromise. Until you walk in another's footsteps, you will find it hard to understand.

*Use sincere praise for work well done. Avoid unworthy flattery.

*Lose yourself in service to others. The covenants are in the first mile; the blessings are in the second mile; the miracles are in the third.

*Embrace the Golden Rule without qualifying it. Keep it in mind always.

*Express real interest in others without invading their personal privacy. Build relationships of trust, even with loved ones and friends.

*Avoid taking people for granted or using them for selfish reasons.

*Try not to polarize situations when differences of opinion exist. Build "win—win" solutions by seeking acceptable compromises or solutions. "Win—win" occurs when everyone involved feels good about the result or decision, and no one loses face with others.

*Overcome natural man tendencies to be defensive, sarcastic, abrasive, or protective of "your own turf."

*Bite off quick, defensive retorts. Think about the effects of your words. When arguments begin, the real reason they started is quickly forgotten and many things are said that have no bearing on what caused the disagreement in the first place.

160   Where Art Thou

*Heal the sorrows of others but avoid competing with them. Our challenge is not to beat our "competitors" but to concentrate on our own performances. You are your own competitor, and frequently your own worst enemy.

ATTRIBUTE NUMBER 7:

GODLINESS: WHAT IS IT?

A substitute word for **godliness** is **goodlikeness** which means to have the good qualities of God in our lives. This is how we achieve the teaching of Elder Lorenzo Snow, *"As man now is, God once was; as God now is, man may become."*

It is the attribute of **godliness** that we inherited from our Eternal Father. It causes us to feel godly sorrow when we transgress our covenants. This sorrow is manifested through the Holy Ghost and prompts us to true repentance. It is often the case that covenant—breakers feel much worse in their sins than those who are not yet members of the Church. " . . .*Wickedness never was happiness"* (see Alma 41:10), to which we could add godliness always brings happiness.

This concept was emphasized by the Lord, *"And withut the ordinances thereof, and the authority of the priesthood, the power of **godliness** is not manifest unto men in the flesh"* (see D&C 84:21). It follows, therefore, that **godliness** consists of two critical components: (1) the covenants we make with God; and (2) being faithful unto the attaining of the priesthood and the magnifying thereof (see D&C 84:33).

The importance of these two components is shown by Christ, *"For without this, no man can see the face of God, even the Father, and live"* (see D&C 84:22). To live to see God is the purpose of acquiring **godliness**. Since no unclean thing can dwell in His presence, to acquire this attribute we must become justified and sanctified. Is it any wonder then that each sin we commit moves us away from God, a lessening in our

Chapter 1   161

feeling of **godliness**, and a corresponding increase in our sense of guilt and remorse and shame? Thus enters the Law of Justice.

GODLINESS: HOW TO ACQUIRE IT

*Become a frequent participant in all of the temple ordinances. Each time you do work for others (brotherly kindness), you vicariously renew your understanding of your own covenants, and you enlarge your knowledge of their meanings, if you attend with the right attitude.

*Avoid pleasures that conflict with **godliness**. Attending unclean activities and listening to immoral music and jokes causes us to be despisers of good, because repetition breaks down our resistance.

*Shun profanity and vulgarity. Avoid taking the name of God in vain for *any* reason.

*Raise your friends to your level of **godliness**; never descend to theirs.

*Keep your conversations clean, uplifting, and holy.

*Replace evil thoughts immediately when they are recalled to your memory. Keep a supply of good thoughts at your fingertips for this purpose.

*Avoid contentions. The Holy Ghost departs when contentions occur. Obedience and love brings peace and **godliness.**

*Honor and magnify the priesthood in all of your actions.

ATTRIBUTE NUMBER 8:

CHARITY: WHAT IS IT?

Of all the Christ—like attributes, **charity** appears to have the clearest scriptural definition. It is always expressed as the

162   Where Art Thou

pure love of Christ, and that makes it the highest, strongest, and deepest kind of love that we can possibly feel for anyone. The Savior frequently associated **charity** with helping those less fortunate than ourselves. This portrays true Christianity in action.

Charity is the willingness to do things for others without expecting something in return. It has to be completely and totally voluntary, and, therefore, it becomes the sweetest of all fruit as Lehi's vision tells us. His whole soul was filled with the most desirable of feelings because he was flooded with sweet charity in his concern for his wayward children.

It was the acquisition and development of this depth of love that prepared those living in the City of Enoch to be translated. *"And the Lord called his people Zion, because they were of **one heart and one mind,** and dwelt in righteousness; and there was no poor among them"* (see Moses 7:18). **Charity** and poverty, economic or spiritual, do not co—exist in God's Kingdom. There is no other way by which such oneness in heart and in mind can be obtained in the family of Christ.

CHARITY: HOW TO ACQUIRE IT

*Ponder and adopt the positive characteristics in this scripture, *"And **charity** suffereth long, and is kind, and envieth not, and is not puffed up, seeketh not her own, is not easily provoked, thinketh no evil, and rejoiceth not in iniquity but rejoiceth in the truth, beareth all things, believeth all things, hopeth all things, endureth all things"* (see Moroni 7:45).

*Perform acts of service untainted by an expected return, *"And behold, I tell you these things that ye may learn wisdom; that ye may learn that when ye are in the service of your fellow beings ye are only in the service of your God"* (see Mosiah 2:17).

*Put aside thoughts of your own comfort when faced with

Chapter 1   163

a choice of whether or not to help others.

*Love your enemies and do good things for those who use you.

*Pray for those who need you and bless those who curse you (see D&C 12:8;18:19).

*Purify your thoughts. Be proactive in keeping them clean.

*Do not support any form of wickedness even though you are a non—participant. Wrong will always be wrong in any situation.

*Refrain from putting down others who are trying to do what is right. Help them instead.

*Be obedient to each and every commandment and covenant, then comes love and **charity**, which can only be achieved and maintained when your love for Christ and His children is unconditional, eternal, and perfect (see 2 Nephi 26:30; Moroni 7:47; Moroni 8:25—26).

ATTRIBUTE NUMBER 9:

HUMILITY: WHAT IS IT?

The antithesis of **humility** is pride. Proud individuals do not change their attitudes or behaviors when they are shown to be wrong. Rather, they rationalize and defend their positions. Sometimes such people perceive this attribute as a sign of weakness because they associate it with being timid; to be timid is to show fear.

In reality, we can be powerful and courageous, yet humble all at the same time. This is possible because the true definition of this attribute is to completely recognize our relationship to our Heavenly Father at all times, and to respond to His holy

164   Where Art Thou

will without question, fear, hesitation, or argument. It is very possible that the truest form of **humility** goes hand—in—hand with living the Law of Consecration.

To possess **humility** is to eschew pride, personal selfishness, and comparing yourself with others. Such comparisons always show you at your worst and others at their best. It is impossible to be humble in Christ when our attention is centered on the things of the world which frequently provide the basis for negative selfish behaviors.

This attribute recognizes a complete dependence on the Lord. It admits that, without His help, we cannot succeed in our quest for exaltation, and that, with His help, we cannot fail. *"Be thou humble; and the Lord thy God shall lead thee by the hand, and give thee answer to thy prayers"* (see D&C 112:10). Imagine being led by the Lord who is holding your hand! What an incentive for us to acquire this attribute!

HUMILITY: HOW TO ACQUIRE IT

*Recognize and give thanks for the part that the Savior plays in answering our prayers and guiding us in our accomplishments. He is our tutor and He will take us by the hand, even in our prayers, if we have **humility.**

*Embark on your own journey towards full and complete justification by repenting of your sins, including confession and restitution, where possible.

*Ensure that your prayers are sincere and honest. Learn to hold a spiritual discussion with your Father just as you would with your best friend.

*Seek the applause of God. He is so very anxious to help us move as fast as we possibly can towards sanctification. The pace is ours to set.

Chapter 1

*Desire to acquire this attribute with all your heart. *"And now, as I said unto you, that because ye were compelled to be humble ye were blessed, do ye not suppose that they are more blessed who truly humble themselves because of the word? Yea, he that truly humbleth himself, and repenteth of his sins, and endureth to the end, the same shall be blessed — yea, much more blessed than they who are compelled to be humble because of their exceeding poverty"* (see Alma 32:14—15).

*Remember to always return thanks to God for all your blessings. There is very little of eternal worth you can achieve without His help.

*Develop as strong a loyalty for the Savior as He did for the Father. In order to really do this, we must use funnel vision in our view of the basic commandments and covenants of God.

*Consecrate your entire life to the Father. The greater your interdependence with the Godhead, the closer you will approach perfect **humility.**

ATTRIBUTE NUMBER 10:

DILIGENCE: WHAT IS IT?

In a Gospel sense, this Christ—like attribute consists of enduring to the end. This would include perseverance, dedication, a strong work ethic, a dogged determination to overcome trials and adversities, and an eagerness to listen to counsel and take advice from Church leaders.

James instructed us to *"But be ye doers of the word, and not hearers only, deceiving your own selves"* (see James 1:22). To accomplish this, we must have **diligence** which President Ezra Taft Benson has equated with hard work. He taught that there is no satisfactory substitute for work, work, work.

Such a work ethic would result in teaching with **diligence**

166   Where Art Thou

to avoid answering the sins of others on our own heads (see Jacob 1:19); searching out our records (see Mosiah 1:7); being diligent in keeping the commandments (see D&C 6:20); and gaining more knowledge and intelligence in order to have an advantage in the world to come (see D&C 130:19). All of these instructions strongly suggest that God's most valuable blessings are in the second mile for it takes little **diligence** to only travel the first one.

DILIGENCE: HOW TO ACQUIRE IT

*Conform your life to the divine will of your Heavenly Father because you love Him without reservation; not because it is your duty as His child.

*Commit yourself to complete your journey all the way to Exaltation. Resolve that there will be no side roads or detours or intermediate stops as you proceed. Jesus taught the Nephites: *"Verily, verily, I say unto you, this is my gospel; and ye know the things that ye must do in my church; for the works which ye have seen me do that shall ye also do; for that which ye have seen me do even that shall ye do"* (see 3 Nephi 27:21).

*Persevere in your steadfastness in Christ. *"Search diligently, pray always, and be believing, and all things shall work together for your good, if ye walk uprightly and remember the covenant wherewith ye have covenanted one with another"* (see D&C 90:24).

*Become a truly spiritual person who has no priorities ahead of God.

*Be prepared to climb mountains. There will be trials, tribulations, and adversities in our lives but we cannot be discouraged because of them We cannot become as pure as gold and as clean as the freshly fallen snow unless we are diligent in pressing forward towards the mark for the prize offered through the atonement of Christ.

Chapter 1　　　　　167

ATTRIBUTE NUMBER 11:

POWER: WHAT IS IT?

When we speak of this attribute, we frequently refer to the control or influence that we have or exercise over other people and events. We also use it to indicate by what authority we bless others. In another sense, **power** is knowledge properly applied to daily living.

Power becomes the moving cause of all of our actions. Because of the powerful influences we can wield on others, the Lord was concerned that we use it prudently and wisely. For example, Korihor's sins were compounded by the fact that " . . .*he did preach unto them, leading away the hearts of many . . .*" (see Alma 30:18).

Power in the Gospel is the ability to act in behalf of Jesus Christ and to do His will in righteousness and under His direction. To exercise power in this manner, we are required to know the will of the Lord, use our intelligence in wisely applying that will of the Lord, and demonstrate faith in dedicated service. *"But the Lord knoweth all things from the beginning; wherefore, he prepareth a way to accomplish all his works among the children of men; for behold, he hath all power unto the fulfilling of all his words..."* (see 1 Nephi 9:6).

POWER: HOW TO ACQUIRE IT

*Exercise righteous **power** over yourself first; then you can better help others.

*Purify your methods, techniques, and reasons for living the Gospel. Your **power** over yourself will increase with each purification.

*Sort out your true desires. These initiate your actions and sustain you either for good or evil. If you desire to be like

168   Where Art Thou

Christ, then you will develop the necessary course of action based on obedience. The discipleship of Christ is for volunteers only and you must be the one that makes that commitment for yourself.

*Develop an exceptionally sharp and sensitive conscience. The exercise of **power** over yourself requires it. To do this, you must be meek and humble and clean, thus being worthy at all times for a constant, perfect partnership with the Holy Ghost.

*Accept the fact that you can only influence others in your problems by involving them in meaningful ways. If you "use" people, you exercise unrighteous dominion because you really have no intention of accepting their suggestions, only in passing the burden for your problems on to their shoulders.

*Improve the basis on which **power** exists in your Christ—like life and you will increase your feeling of being in charge of your life. This basis includes, but is not limited to, love, faith, knowledge, intelligence, long—suffering, meekness, and kindness.

ATTRIBUTE NUMBER 12:

JUSTICE: WHAT IS IT?

In its broadest sense, **justice** means fairness and impartiality. In its use by the Lord, we have come to understand that every time He gives us a commandment, He tells us what is required of us, explains the blessings that we can earn if we are obedient to it, and states the punishment that must be meted out if we disobey His commandments.

The plain fact is that every time a law is broken or a commandment not kept a penalty is required. Some-

Chapter 1   169

one must pay for those acts of transgression. That is the essence of the Law of **Justice.**

Because of the Atonement of Christ, the Savior has paid the penalty for every law we break *if we properly repent*, thus involving the Law of Mercy. If we do not properly repent, **we must suffer even as he did** (see D&C 19:17). He said, *"For I the Lord cannot look upon sin with the least degree of allowance"* (see D&C1:31).

However, the quality of that **justice** is not for us to decide. True **justice** is that which conforms to the mind and will of the Redeemer. It must be righteous and proper before Him. The transgression and the penalty are of equal value. One is not less than nor greater than the other. Otherwise, God would be unfair and unjust.

This attribute centers on fairness: *"If a person does not perform a particular commandment because he is genuinely unable to do so, but truly would if he could, our Heavenly Father will know this, and will reward that person accordingly"* (see Dallin H. Oaks, *Pure in Heart*, p. 13). What could be more fair?

In view of this eternal law, it is false doctrine to assume that, because God loves us without reservation, He will overlook our little sins, particularly if we repent of the bigger ones. The application of the Law of **Justice** demands a penalty, and only true repentance or Christ's Atonement meets that demand. As quoted earlier, He will not, indeed cannot, pay the penalty if we fail to repent. Thus, we, not the Lord, place ourselves in the grasp of **justice.**

JUSTICE: HOW TO ACQUIRE IT

*Have as much compassion for others as you want from them or that you want from the Lord. *"Shouldest not thou also have compassion on the fellowservant, even as I had pity on thee?"* (see Matthew 18:33).

170　　　　　　　Where Art Thou

*Convince yourself that it is far better to abstain from transgression than to have to repent. Many negative experiences need to have never been shared if we had followed a policy of prevention. *We simply do not have to sin.*

*Understand that there is a difference between err and error. To err is to fail to act or to have acted incorrectly without wrongful intent. Such errs will be made known to us, and we will be taught correct behavior by our loving Brother and Tutor. To commit an error is to do so intentionally after we have been so taught. Repentance is required for all errors (see Dallin H. Oaks, *Pure in Heart*, p.34).

*Study the Atonement of the Lord profoundly. An understanding of this doctrine will give us many reasons to abstain from sin or to repent of those already committed.

*Be assured that we cannot escape the "all—seeing eye of God." We can never hide even the smallest sin from Him.

*Have faith in the just and fair judgments of the Savior. He will not exact from us more than is required. *"For I, the Lord, will judge all men according to their works, according to the desires of their hearts"* (see D&C 137:9).

*Apply the Golden Rule and the Lord's Prayer proactively in your life. This will help to prevent many transgressions from even beginning. *"And forgive us our debts, as we forgive our debtors. But if ye forgive not men their trespasses, neither will your Father forgive your trespasses"* (see Matthew 6:12,15). Why would there be a need to forgive if there were no trespasses?

ATTRIBUTE NUMBER 13:

JUDGMENT: WHAT IS IT?

Judgment is the ability to make wise and righteous

Chapter 1   171

decisions followed by the carrying out of those decisions to successful conclusions. Unless we comprehend the teachings already given on perceptions, our **judgments** may frequently be suspect because they will be based on incorrect perceptions rooted in incomplete data.

God's **judgment**, on the other hand, is perfect because He knows all things. His data is complete. His perceptions are accurate. *"He is the Rock, his work is perfect: for all his ways are **judgment**: a God of truth and without iniquity, just and right is he"* (see Deuteronomy 32:4).

God judges us wisely and righteously for what we do as well as for what we would do righteously if we had been given the opportunity. This is His responsibility. Likewise, it is our responsibility to make righteous **judgments**, and then to carry them out. This action step is required in order for us to demonstrate our sincerity and our willingness to pay the price for that which is of the greatest worth to us.

JUDGMENT: HOW TO ACQUIRE IT

*Develop your powers of discernment and understanding so that your decisions and actions will be based on corrected perceptions. Discernment is a gift of the Holy Ghost for which you should pray continually. This beautiful gift will help you cut through many false symptoms directly to the problem itself. Then, your **judgments** will be so much more accurate.

*Check your **judgments**. Be sure your motives for judging are Christ—like. "Judge not unrighteously, that ye be not judged: but judge righteous **judgment**" (see JST Matthew 7:2).

*Carry out your righteous **judgments**. You have covenanted with the Lord to do, not to refrain from doing, virtuous deeds. Doing looks forward and upward, provides incentives on which to base further wise decisions, and gives vitality to overcoming faults and mistaken perceptions.

172   Where Art Thou

*Assume full responsibility for the cleanliness of your thoughts. These frequently are the cause of quick, hasty, poor **judgments**. Purify your thoughts, then purify your decisions, thus purifying your actions.

*Think before you act. If you can do this difficult step, many problems and errors would never even occur.

ATTRIBUTE NUMBER 14:

MERCY: WHAT IS IT?

To posses **mercy**, one needs to demonstrate a willingness to spare another unnecessary pain or suffering. To grant forgiveness or clemency is also a part of this attribute in dealing with others.

This Christ—like attribute is all too often lost in a discussion of the Law of Justice, and vice versa. We so desire the reward, we tend to overlook the price to be paid or the process to be followed, including involving a Priesthood leader where specified by the Lord.

We have absolutely no claim on the **mercy** of the Savior until we have both paid the price of full, complete repentance, and followed the process outlined by Him who has earned the right to dispense this attribute by virtue of His sacrifices in both the Garden of Gethsemane and on the cross of Calvary. *"And now, the plan of mercy could not be brought about except an atonement should be made: therefore God himself atoneth for the sins of the world, to bring about the plan of mercy, to appease the demands of justice, that God might be a perfect, just God, and a merciful God also"* (see Alma 42:15).

Mercy is therefore an attribute of God. It is based on His grace, love, and condescension as well as on our complete repentance. The only general sense in which it is applied is in overcoming the effects of the fall brought about by Adam and

Eve. It is by virtue of the overcoming that all can be resurrected. All other applications of **mercy** applied to us by the Savior is on a sin—by—sin basis, if we repent.

This Christ—like attribute is also required of us. The Lord commanded, *"Be ye therefore merciful, as your Father also is merciful"* (see Luke 6:36).

In a Gospel sense, **mercy** is the opportunity Jesus gives us to repent but we must also forgive others of their trespasses against us. Can we develop a deep appreciation for the sacrifice of the Savior without then applying it to others? To do so would result in a hardened heart. *"Therefore, whosoever repenteth and hardeneth not his heart, he shall have claim on **mercy** through mine Only Begotten Son, unto a remission of his sins; and these shall enter into my rest"* (see Alma 12:34).

MERCY: HOW TO ACQUIRE IT

*Become hungry enough for this attribute to want to acquire it now. To be that hungry, you must center your life on Christ and keep His commandments with deep faith and abiding love. *"For they have been faithful over many things, and have done well inasmuch as they have not sinned. Behold, I, the Lord, am merciful and will bless them, and they shall enter into the joy of these things . . ."* (see D&C 70:17—18).

*Search your life for unresolved transgressions. Take care of these now, but understand that there will be ones — long forgotten — that you cannot recall, no matter how hard you try. If you are personally righteous and pure in heart, the Lord will grant you forgiveness and **mercy**. This is what He meant when He said, *"I, the Lord, will forgive whom I will forgive, but of you it is required to forgive all men"* (see D&C 64:10). Such forgiveness from the Lord is based on His **mercy**.

*Show **mercy** to those with whom you associate — members or not. This consists of compassion, forbearance,

174   Where Art Thou

self—control, and tolerance. *"Be ye therefore merciful, as your Father also is merciful"* (see Luke 6:36).

*"*Sow to yourselves in righteousness, reap in* **mercy** *...*" (see Hosea 10:12). The Law of the Harvest is very plain and simple — we reap only what we sow. If we want to reap **mercy**, we must first sow it.

*Continue to work on your personal justification in Christ through the Holy Ghost. As you do so, your concept of this attribute will multiply greatly, because you will feel it looming larger and larger in your life. This, in turn, will increase other Christ—like attributes, such as meekness and humility.

ATTRIBUTE NUMBER 15:

TRUTH: WHAT IS IT?

The simplest and most straight forward definition of **truth** was given to us by the Lord: *"And truth is knowledge of things as they are, and as they were, and as they are to come"* (see D&C 93:24; Jacob 4:13). By this definition, **truth** is constant, not relative; an idea which is contrary to many of today's worldly philosophies.

What is relative is our understanding of **truth**. As we learn and understand more **truth**, our comprehension enlarges causing us to revise what we were so sure was true before.

The reverse is also accurate. The law of the spiritual world is that when we shut our minds to **truth**, darkness sets in. Soon, it becomes difficult to believe in anything. Then, we reject God for we have also lost our faith. This is accompanied by a fear of **truth**.

We should not fear the **truth**, only its misuse by careless and wicked people. Given enough time and study, we will find that **truth** will prove itself. Despite "profound" writers and

Chapter 1   175

philosophers, **truth** will still be **truth**, honesty will still be honesty, and God will still be God.

Our search for **truth** must involve a very constructive use of our minds, our bodies, and our spirits. In order to have a highly successful life, we must establish and maintain constant pursuit of all truth. The accumulation of knowledge is not something that can be done for us by other people. We must do it individually for ourselves. *"And ye shall know the **truth**, and the **truth** shall make you free"* (see John 8:32). Too many times, one spouse will lean on the other to do all of the learning and studying. This is a fatal error. One person cannot become intelligent for another.

The Lord has provided us with a great deal of help in our searchings. This help not only assists us with sources, but also with the means to discern **truth**. The Master's provisions include scriptures, personal revelation, the Holy Ghost, temple ordinances, living prophets, the Holy Priesthood, and an intuitive sense of right and wrong. *"But God hath revealed them unto us by his Spirit; for the Spirit searcheth all things, yea, the deep things of God"* (see 1 Corinthians 2:10).

TRUTH: HOW TO ACQUIRE IT

*Desire the **truth** enough to search for it diligently by study. However, you should conduct your search in appropriate places. You will seldom find it in negative resources, but you will find it in many places and subjects.

*Pray for confirmation of those facts which you study. See them as connecting parts of the overall pattern of the revealed Gospel. Avoid thinking of them as isolated pieces of information. Use funnel vision to help with this.

*Use the Holy Ghost to obtain confirmation or denial. That is your privilege as a member of the Church. *"And again, he that receiveth the word of **truth**, doth he receive it by the*

176 Where Art Thou

*Spirit of **truth** or some other way? If it be some other way it is not of God"* (see D&C 50:19—20).

*Learn to love the **truth** above all else. If you love God, you have to love **truth** for God is **truth**. *"Jesus saith unto him, I am the way, the **truth**, and the life; no man cometh unto the Father, but by me"* (see John 14:6). Since God is **truth**, we must not knowingly compromise it; for if we do, we will draw further away from Him. To become sanctified, we must move ever closer to the Savior; therefore, we must search for and practice **truth** in all places and at all times.

*Be true to yourself and to your Heavenly Father. Integrity and **truth** are holy companions. Others need to be able to trust your word and rely on your doing what you have promised to do.

ATTRIBUTE NUMBER 16:

MEEKNESS: WHAT IS IT?

Perhaps this Christ—like attribute would often escape our attention were it not for the fact that the Master personally drew notice to it in the Sermon on the Mount. He repeated that instruction during His visit to the Nephites on the American Continent: *"And blessed are the meek, for they shall inherit the earth"* (see Matthew 5:4; 3 Nephi 12:5).

Worldly people often describe a meek person as one who is without courage or spirit. Obviously, the Lord has a much different definition, else why would He be willing to promise the meek that they would inherit the earth? Our scriptures tell us that this earth will eventually become the Celestial Kingdom.

By offering such a reward, the Master would not define a meek person as one who is fearful, spiritless, or timid. He described Himself as meek and lowly, *"Take my yoke upon*

Chapter 1   177

*you, and learn of me; for I am meek and lowly in heart: and ye
shall find rest unto your souls"* (see Matthew 11:29).

So, what is the Savior's definition of **meekness**? It is to be
godfearing and personally righteous, and to conform to all
gospel standards of your own free will and choice. Therefore,
to be meek is to stand strong in all places and under any
pressures for the right reasons. In meeting this definition, we
can serve God with all of our hearts, mights, minds, and
strengths despite any enticements that Satan or any human
being would offer us to do otherwise.

Meekness means to love Jesus Christ so much that we will
never want Him to suffer for any of our sins. With this attitude,
we would abstain from sin. Displaying such strength will
edify us in our **meekness** (see D&C 84:106), so that it would
become as strong as bands of steel and as pure as fine gold.

MEEKNESS: HOW TO ACQUIRE IT

*Develop a strong sense of your limitations. Work
to strengthen them and to push or extend them outward.
Never permit yourself to be tempted beyond your power
to resist and overcome.

*Walk in the grace of God so that you can always be
spiritually enlightened and strengthened by the Holy
Ghost. This will allow you to avoid transgressions
before you are even tempted.

*Find wonderful, spiritual comfort in the revelations
of God by studying them daily even to the point of
continually finding hidden treasures of knowledge and
wisdom. God is found in His revelations.

*Be completely willing to conform your life to all Gospel
standards, not just a comfortable selection. Take God's word
for it until you can prove it for yourself.

178   Where Art Thou

*Submit your will to that of the Savior. He gave us all. How much are we willing to give in return? You are the only one who can provide yourself with an answer.

ATTRIBUTE NUMBER 17

SUBMISSIVENESS: WHAT IS IT?

To be submissive is to yield ourselves to the will or to the authority of another. In a Gospel sense, the Christ—like attributes of meekness and **submissiveness** must necessarily go hand—in—hand. Unless we are meek, we will not be submissive, and if we are not submissive, we will not be meek.

In his marvelous, powerful discourse, King Benjamin connected **submissiveness** to other attributes of Christ. After speaking about the natural man, he proceeded to tell us to put him off and " . . .*becometh a saint through the atonement of Christ the Lord, and becometh as a child, submissive, meek, humble, patient, full of love, willing to submit to all things which the Lord seeth fit to inflict upon him, even as a child doth submit to his father"* (see Mosiah 3:19).

The opposite of **submissiveness** was described by Paul, *"For they being ignorant of God's righteousness, and going about to establish their own righteousness, having not submitted themselves unto the righteousness of God"* (see Romans 10:3).

Submissiveness helps us to widen and extend our vision of the most fundamental truths, including how we view our purpose in life, and how we develop our personal interdependent relationships with the Holy Trinity. If we successfully establish such relationships, being submissive will assist us make and keep righteous resolutions and dissolve improper pride.

As in all Christ—like attributes, **submissiveness** must be initiated by our personal desires to become like Him of our

Chapter 1   179

own free will and choice. Once we have adequately demonstrated our righteous desires, then we must seek an endowment of assistance from the Savior. It is in this act of seeking Divine help that we express our need for becoming interdependent with Him.

Too much independence and dependence works against us having **submissiveness**. Dependent people are afraid to act for themselves or to accept responsibility for their actions. Independent individuals often do not understand the true principle of free agency and when to be submissive to higher authority. They often act as their own authority. Interdependent people go as far as they can righteously go using their own talents and abilities; then they are not afraid to ask for help from the Father, the Son, and the Holy Ghost. This is why this attribute is difficult to acquire. There are far more dependent and independent individuals than there are others.

SUBMISSIVENESS: HOW TO ACQUIRE IT

*Accept Paul's counsel, *"Casting down imaginations, and every high thing that exalteth itself against the knowledge of God, and bringing into captivity every thought to the obedience of Christ"* (see 2 Corinthians 10:5).

*Recognize that all of God's laws, covenants, and commandments are true and just and fair, even if you do not fully understand them yet.

*Accept completely the fact that God does not expect you to obtain your own personal verification of the righteousness of His ways. He does expect you to want to search, to begin the search, to work hard at it, but He will provide the verification through the Holy Ghost.

*Realize that God's rod of iron is His revealed truth. Use the "iron" concept to understand that self—discipline is an absolute in that truth, and you must be as "iron" against untruths.

180   Where Art Thou

*Maintain a sincere trust for your leaders and refrain from looking at their human weaknesses. Expect not perfection in them until you can offer it in return. *"Seeing ye have purified your souls in obeying the truth through the Spirit unto unfeigned love of the brethren, see that ye love one another with a pure heart fervently"* (see 1 Peter 1:22).

*Aim your sight far above natural man's lower ways (see Mosiah 3). Always focus on the spiritual man's higher concepts (see Alma 5), but do it of your own free will and choice.

*Begin to submit your own soul to the right ways, then become more concerned for others than for yourself. Enos first wrestled before the Lord for a remission of his own sins, then sought for blessings upon his brethren, followed by a preservation of the records (see Enos). Sometimes the Lord wants you to stretch yourself as far as possible before He will help you. Like the rubber band, we are not of much use until we are stretched.

*Avoid giving or taking offense because of the poor actions or words of others. Look to your own perceptions first.

*Accept the tutoring experiences provided for you by a loving Savior.

*Center your mind, thoughts, and intellect on Jesus Christ, and be guided by Him in all things. However, you are required to do all that you can do through obedience first, then submit yourself to Him. Free agency does not ever conflict with or reduce the necessity to be submissive to the Holy Trinity.

ATTRIBUTE NUMBER 18:

LOVE: WHAT IS IT?

In the Standard Works, the attribute of **love** is mentioned 448 times, second only to faith (696 times). In almost every instance, we are given to understand that love is the highest

Chapter 1   181

attribute of the human soul, especially when it is encased in charity. This is because it is the deepest of human feelings, not freely given to everyone with the same intensity by us.

Unfortunately, much of today's media has equated love with sexual feelings, responses, and passions. In many instances, they demonstrate that if such feelings are not present, then neither is **love**.

To the "born again" follower of Jesus Christ, this divine attribute may certainly include sexual feelings and passions. These, however, must be contained within the appropriate confines of marriage and directed towards the marriage partner.

The deepest form of **love** is the greatest power in the world because in that depth there is no fear, only complete trust. *"And no one can assist in this work except he shall be humble and full of love, having faith, hope, and charity, being temperate in all things, whatsoever shall be entrusted to his care"* (see D&C 12:8).

Love alone can overcome hate, greed, selfishness, and fear. It can triumph over force and might, when other feelings fail. To accomplish these victories, we must learn to **love** with all of our emotional feelings and devotions. We must avoid demeaning, criticizing, abusing, fault—finding, back—biting, sullenness, and the silent treatment.

It means that we have to be loyal and faithful. It infers that we must communicate openly and freely with those with whom we have differences. It requires us to eschew rancor, bitterness, or a desire to "get even" when hurt. One who truly **loves** as Christ does must avoid the prideful habit of comparison. Such a habit leads to a poor self—image, a sense of persecution, a feeling that others are taking advantage of us, and a separation from those who would and should mean so much to us.

The true disciple of Christ endeavors to develop an attitude of total empathy and **love**. He or she works hard at the

182   Where Art Thou

building of honest relationships of trust in which others can truly feel that empathy and **love**. Such openness of feelings are true reflections of our sincerest attitudes towards those with whom we are associating.

As with all other attributes, the Savior's **love** is our example. His **love** for us is total, absolute, and freely given. We do not ever have to earn that **love**. He is not like us, for He does not withhold His **love** when we misbehave. He was totally submissive to His Father because of the full depth of His **love** for Elohim as well as for each of us. He, therefore, has the right to expect nothing less from each of us.

Love is the foundation upon which all peace and righteousness exists. This includes our feelings towards ourselves, towards all others, and towards the Father, the Son, and the Holy Ghost. *"But if any man **love** God, the same is known of him"* (see 1 Corinthians 8:3). It is known in our eyes, our words, and our deeds.

LOVE: HOW TO ACQUIRE IT

*Be quick to forgive others. Try not to take offense so easily or quickly, especially where none was intended. When you experience a negative reaction, look to your own perceptions first by asking "find out" questions. Thus, you avoid having the wrong perceptions, building up problems, and having unresolved difficulties. Talk them out after you have reviewed your own feelings.

*Subdue your temper. Learn to control it. One way to do this is to require yourself to look for the good in others rather than for hidden agendas. Another is to talk to yourself in private.

*Praise sincerely other people's virtues. Commend their good accomplishments but avoid meaningless flattery, and be slow to criticize.

*Develop a sensitivity towards other people's feelings by

Chapter 1 183

observing their non—verbal communication signals. Eliminate the natural man's defenses of sarcasm, put—downs, sharp retorts, getting even, and hurtful humor.

*Walk away from contentions. The Holy Ghost will never be present during arguments. Do not dispute with others on sensitive subjects.

*Cultivate patience and long—suffering. Learn to "bite your tongue" rather to say something you will regret later. To respond too quickly frequently polarizes the issues and hurts the feelings of those involved, even to the extent that further clarification or resolution may never be effected.

*Express your **love** for others. If you **love** them, tell them. It will amaze you how quickly differences evaporate when **love** is expressed.

*Do things for others without expecting anything in return. In fact, an anonymous service often produces the most peaceful responses your soul could ever hope to have.

*Swallow your pride. Those with whom you associate have most likely been raised differently than you. Their values may be very dissimilar. Do not take offense where none is intended. Examine your own perceptions and values first, then recognize real differences where they honestly exist. You cannot make others over into your image, no matter how much you try.

*Realize how valuable each soul is to Jesus Christ. *"Remember the worth of souls is great in the sight of God"* (see D&C 18:10). This includes your own soul. Self-**love** is not a sin, unless it is carried too far in pride, or of it is immoral.

*Treasure your character and value your reputation by developing **love** and integrity for yourself.

*Remind yourself constantly that true **love** demands ac-

184   Where Art Thou

tion and service. You cannot "profess" **love** without per-
forming positive and virtuous actions that are based on a
desire to lift others up. The ultimate test of Christian **love** is in
deeds done for others based on pure, clean motives.

*Keep in mind that life becomes larger as one's selfish-
ness becomes smaller. Every positive, loving act is a form of
communication that blesses all those involved, and this
includes your own soul.

*Learn to **love** those whom you do not like. Such a sacrifice gives you faith to initiate and sustain improved behavior
in the Lord's work, and it develops your own selfconfidence
to repeat it. These successes then improve your self-esteem
which, in turn, encourages you to reach out to others again and
again. Such a cycle moves you upward ever higher in your
love for self and others. Gradually, you will realize that many
of your "dislikes" were based on insufficient data or false
perceptions. Once this situation changes, your dislikes seem
to also change, usually for the better.

There are a number of other Christ-like attributes which
you might desire to add to this list, such as obedience,
reverence, unity, honesty, accountability, service, self-discipline, and courage - to name a few. No human listing can ever
be complete. You should always be alert to ways in which you
can expand the list as well as improve the quality of the
thoughts provided in this publication.

As you work with the attributes, you are encouraged to do
so in the framework of the ten steps to sanctification(see
Chapter Three, page 32). By following a good plan, you will
arrive at the assurance that, as you improve one attribute, you
will be simultaneously working on several others, perhaps
without being conscious of it.

As with the steps to repentance, your acquisition and
development of these attributes begins with desire. Unfortu-

Chapter 1   185

nately, too many of us are known as "gonna" individuals. We are always "gonna" do it but tomorrow is soon enough to make a start.

It takes hard, directed, and purposeful action to become Christ-like. *"Though he were a Son, yet learned he obedience by the things which he suffered"* (see Hebrews 5:8). We cannot learn very much of eternal value by a lack of action. We may deceive ourselves but never our Righteous Judge. *"Behold, I am the law, and the light. Look unto me, and endure to the end, and ye shall live; for unto him that endureth to the end will I give eternal life"* (see 3 Nephi 15:9).

To "look unto" Christ, we must become like Him. That means we must acquire His attributes. There is no other way. As we become more and more like Christ, we will never misuse or abuse the power of the priesthood which he has entrusted to us. We are invited to come unto Christ so that we can come unto the Father. Righteous use of the priesthood and coming unto Christ are one and the same thing.

186   Where Art Thou

Chapter Fourteen

THE DOCTRINE OF THE PRIESTHOOD

> **D&C 121:45 —** *"Let thy bowels also be full of charity towards all men, and to the household of faith, and let virtue garnish thy thoughts unceasingly; then shall thy confidence wax strong in the presence of God; and the doctrine of the priesthood shall distil upon thy soul as the dews from heaven."*

Some years ago, one of the professional football teams in the National Football League had a disastrous season despite the fact that the players were very high quality and talented. The coach felt that the reason was not in their skills or in the training, but in their attitude.

During the off—season, the staff employed a counselor to work with the players on setting individual goals for their own personal athletic achievements. Then, when the training camp began, he met with the entire team in order to have them set a team goal. This they did. The goals they unanimously agreed to work towards for the entire season were to go unbeaten in every game and to get into the Super Bowl.

The season was a tremendous success. The team did, in fact, go undefeated in every game — an accomplishment very seldom achieved. Needless to say, the team was the prohibitive favorite to win the Super Bowl. But, in that championship

188   Where Art Thou

game, they were soundly thrashed by the underdog competition.

After the bitterness of the terrible defeat began to wear off, an analysis of the reasons why it happened was made. Following many hours of debate and discussion, it was finally concluded that the major reason for the great loss was that the team had aimed too low. They had set their goal to get into the Super Bowl, not to win it — but just to get into it. Had they aimed higher at winning that game, they may very well have accomplished it and emerged as the winners. As it was, they had achieved their original goal, even though it was not what they really wanted.

Many of us are just like that team. We have great ambitions, vibrant energies, and high goals. But, are we centered on the correct and highest purposes? It does not take much experience in working with other people to arrive at one inescapable conclusion — that on whatever we direct or focus our primary attention, we will achieve it; and it will control, even dominate, our lives.

It is also evident that many of our successes and failures are tied very closely to our emotions, which in turn drive our actions. If our goal is a high one, we will generally be in greater control of our emotions. This will ensure that our actions are directed more precisely and purposefully towards the accomplishment of our goal.

For example, the football team's goals were to go undefeated and to get into the Super Bowl. The emotions of the team were very high, especially as one win followed another. Their actions were such that they won each game in a variety of different ways. These demonstrated both their skills as football players working closely together, and their abilities to proactively make things happen for the benefit of the team. Thus, they accomplished their goals. They did go undefeated and they did get into the Super Bowl.

The Prophet Joseph Smith lived a long time before that

Chapter 1   189

football team was ever thought of, but he knew the psychology of the human race. It has not changed. He demonstrated that knowledge in the verse of scripture quoted at the beginning of this chapter. Joseph Smith said that we must be full of charity towards all men and to the household of faith. Further, he told us that our virtue should garnish our thoughts unceasingly.

On another occasion, the Prophet stated, *"As you increase in innocence and virtue, as you increase in goodness, let your hearts expand, let them be enlarged towards others* [charity]; *you must be long—suffering* [virtue] *and bear with the faults and errors of mankind* [faith]" (see *Teachings of the Prophet Joseph Smith*, page 228).

We have seen from our example of the football team that, when a goal is set too low, the corresponding emotions and actions are also too low. Since our Prophet speaks for the Father, his instructions have to be in keeping with the Father's purposes and plans.

No secret has ever been made of the fact that our Heavenly Father wants us to return to His presence to live with Him forever. That is the goal which we have set for ourselves and which He has offered to us.

This return is the highest goal that each of us can ever achieve. Since it is, then the emotions and actions outlined for us by the Prophet Joseph Smith should be ours also, and they must be of the highest order possible if we are to achieve our appointed goal.

In fact, after Adam and Eve had partaken of the fruit of the Tree of Knowledge of Good and Evil, the Father exacted promises from them that they would always be obedient to His commandments and sacrifice their lives to serve Him. Because these promises were freely given by Adam and Eve (who truly understood the Gospel plan), Elohim promised to them a Savior who would provide for them the way by which they could

190   Where Art Thou

overcome their sins and return to live with the Father forever.

What are the emotions and actions outlined for us by Joseph Smith? He said that they included charity, faith, and virtue. By cultivating these emotions, they will shape and direct our attitudes and behaviors. The repetitiveness of these will cause our confidence to wax strong in the presence of God. Thus, the doctrine of the priesthood distils upon our souls, and this constitutes the actions we must take to fulfill this ultimate of all goals.

You should take strong notice that the emotions of charity, faith, and virtue are action feelings. They must come from within us through our giving of them to others. This is most profoundly demonstrated in the life of Jesus. *"And a certain woman, which had an issue of blood twelve years, and had suffered many things of many physicians, and had spent all that she had, and was nothing bettered, but rather grew worse, when she had heard of Jesus, came in the press behind, and touched his garment. For she said, If I may touch but his clothes, I shall be whole. And straightway the fountain of her blood was dried up; and she felt in her body that she was healed of that plague. And Jesus, immediately knowing in himself that **virtue** had gone out of him, turned him about in the press, and said, Who touched my clothes?" . . ."And he said unto her, Daughter, thy **faith** hath made thee whole; go in peace, and be whole of thy plague"* (see Mark 5:25—34).

To clarify what we have discussed so far, the goal is Exaltation in the Celestial Kingdom, not just entrance into the Celestial Kingdom (to aim for this lower goal is to do what the football team did). The emotions that we need to cultivate in order to attain this highest of goals are charity, faith, and virtue. The actions we need to perform are to encompass these emotions in the righteous use of the Holy Priesthood.

There should be no question in your mind about that higher goal. *"And this is life eternal, that they might know thee*

Chapter 1   191

the only true God, and Jesus Christ, whom thou has sent" (see John 17:3). Joseph Smith enlarged upon this when he said, *"Here, then, is eternal life — to know the only wise and true God; and you have got to learn how to be gods yourselves, and to be kings and priests to God, the same as all gods have done before you, namely, by going from one small degree to another, and from a small capacity to a great one"* (See *History of the Church*, 6:306).

To know our true and living Heavenly Father is only possible if we earn the right to live with Him. There is no other alternative offered to us. *"No man can know the Father and the Son who does not dwell in their presence. Those who do dwell in their presence and have partaken of the fulness of the covenants and who have proved themselves worthy, shall be like God, for they are the sons and daughters of God, and numbered as the members of his grand family"* (President Joseph Fielding Smith).

This same process also occurs in satisfying marriages. As the husband and wife live each day for each other in the embrace of Gospel principles, they come to understand each other in greater and deeper ways. Such a couple realizes that love is a process, not a destination. By doing loving and kind things for each other, they really begin to know each other. By continually following these procedures, their love and their lives become eternal.

Now that we have firmly established our ultimate goal, and there can be no higher one, let us examine the emotions we need to acquire and use in order to reach that goal. We have already considered the fact that the emotions include charity, faith, and virtue. We detailed these Christ—like attributes in the last chapter. You may want to refresh your memory of those details. We now need to understand why these were selected in this scripture to represent the highest emotions necessary to reach our high goal.

It is a rather interesting phenomenon that we attach perfect

192   Where Art Thou

attributes to the Father and the Son. For example, we certainly
expect the Godhead to be unqualified in their charity towards
us. If there should be any doubts raised by our actions, we most
definitely feel that the Father should give us the benefit of that
doubt. We pray for, and expect to receive, every blessing that
we feel we deserve. Usually, we are impatient for its arrival.

But, when it comes to the exercise of unqualified charity
on our part, we are usually quite content to give much less than
our best. In fact, we compound our problems by rationalizing
that, since we are less than perfect, such failures are not only
understandable, they are acceptable to both ourselves and
God. The same logic can easily be applied towards the
attributes of faith and virtue.

A parallelism can be made relative to such community
actions as the closing of a school. We can readily accept the
fact that, because of declining enrollments, a school needs to
be closed. But, close "their" school and keep ours open.

This is a far cry from the way it should be. In fact, it is a
double—standard situation. *"It is one thing to know about
God and another to know him. We know about him when we
learn that he is a personal being in whose image man was
created; when we learn that the Son is in the express image of
his Father's person; when we learn that both the Father and
the Son possess certain specified attributes and powers. But
we know them, in the sense of gaining eternal life, when we
enjoy and experience the same things they do. To know God
is to think what he thinks, to feel what he feels, to have the power
he possesses, to comprehend the truths he understands, and to do
what he does. **Those who know God become like him**, and have
his kind of life, which is eternal life"* (Joseph Fielding Smith).

Can any instruction be plainer or stronger than this from
one of Christ's Apostles? In the development and acquisition
of the Christ—like attributes of charity, faith, and virtue, we
must use the standards established for us by the Father and the

Chapter 1   193

Son. How else could we do as Joseph Fielding Smith states —
think as He thinks, experience what He experiences, and feel
as He feels? This means, of course, that our personal definitions of these attributes simply will not measure up unless they
coincide exactly with the Father's.

If they do, we will have the power [the priesthood] He has,
comprehend what He understands, and do what He does. Our
lives would change vastly in many positive ways if we set
aside our weak rationalizations regarding our human imperfections and set our feet on a non—hypocritical acquisition on
these attributes and this basis.

In the Savior's own words, *"Behold, I am the law, and the
light. **Look unto me**, and endure to the end, and ye shall live
. . ."* (see 3 Nephi 15:9). To look unto Christ is to love Him
with all of our hearts, souls, minds, and strengths. It is indeed
unfortunate that many men and women are willing to die for
Christ, but relatively few are willing to truly live for Him. If
we were completely serious about living for the Savior, we
would be equally as serious about becoming as perfect as we
can be in faith, charity, virtue, and all the rest of His attributes.
Then, we live as He lives, and all other blessings will flow
towards us. These include the proactive feeling that **we are the
master of our souls, and we love how we feel about that.**

Earlier we said that the action we need to use in reaching
our ultimate goal is the proper and righteous use of the
priesthood. To understand the truth of that statement, we need
to examine the doctrine of the priesthood as compared to the
rights of the priesthood discussed in previous chapters.

*"The priesthood is the rule and government of God,
whether on earth or in heaven; and it is the only legitimate
power, the only authority that is acknowledged by Him to rule
and regulate the affairs of His kingdom. It is the power of God
delegated to man by which man can act in the earth for the
salvation of the human family in the name of the Father and*

194   Where Art Thou

the Son and the Holy Ghost, and act legitimately; not assuming that authority, not borrowing it from generations that are dead and gone, but authority that has been given in this day in which we live by ministering angels and spirits from above, direct from the presence of Almighty God" (President Joseph F. Smith, *Gospel Doctrine*, pp. 139—140).

In the verse of scripture quoted at the beginning of this chapter, we were told that if we were full of charity, faith, and virtue, our confidence would wax strong in the presence of God, and the doctrine of the priesthood would distil upon our souls as the dews from heaven. Given the beautiful concept of the power and majesty of the priesthood, as stated by President Joseph F. Smith above, does it not seem to be ambiguous that it should distil as dew upon our souls under any other basis that the Father and the Son have laid down for us through their Prophet, the President of the Church?

To properly assume that question, we need to comprehend what is meant by the term "doctrine of the priesthood" — and you have to search long and hard for an explanation. You can look up the words "doctrine" and "priesthood" and find a great amount of information. However, when you search for the combination "doctrine of the priesthood," your efforts are much less satisfying.

The following explanation is offered for your consideration. You will need to study, ponder, and pray for your own satisfaction. These thoughts are based upon the conclusion that the doctrine of the priesthood comprises several composite concepts, rather than just a simple definition. These concepts are as follows:

*The priesthood is the eternal power and authority of God by which all things exist (see D&C 84:17—21).

*It is only by the authority of the priesthood that the ordinances of the Gospel can be administered *and received* by members of the true Church (see D&C 84:29—30; D&C 107:5). These ordinances comprise the rights of the priest-

Chapter 1

hood as discussed in Chapter Eleven.

*No one can hold an office in the priesthood without first receiving the authority of the priesthood. This is the reason why a male member has the appropriate priesthood bestowed upon him before he is ordained to a particular office within that priesthood. The ordinance used in doing that must be authorized, in advance, by the appropriate presiding authority. For example, a father cannot ordain his son to the office of a deacon unless he is given permission to do that by the Bishop in advance. His fathership is insufficient authority for him to do it on his own. By comparison, in giving a father's blessing, he needs no permission.

*The keys of the priesthood are all active in only one man at a time. That man is the Prophet and President of the Church of Jesus Christ of Latter—Day Saints. He is authorized to delegate those keys, as appropriate, so that every act that is performed by the authority of the priesthood will be done at the proper time and place, in the proper manner, and after the prescribed order. Thus, the stake president receives the keys to preside over his own stake and the High Priest Quorum within that stake. He cannot preside over any other stake. He must receive these keys from one who has the authority to bestow them.

*When properly authorized by one who holds the correct key, a priesthood holder blesses the lives of others, establishes order in the Church unit for which he is responsible, and acts for and in behalf of the Savior within the limits of his prescribed authority for that unit, organization, or quorum.

*In accepting the priesthood, a man solemnly agrees to magnify his calling in the priesthood, to keep the commandments, to live by every word that proceeds from the mouth of God through His prophets, and to walk uprightly in virtue, righteousness, charity, faith, and all other Christ—like attributes.

*In return, God agrees to give to every person, who is so obedient, an inheritance of exaltation and godhood in His

196   Where Art Thou

everlasting presence. This makes the priesthood covenant an eternal covenant for righteous man is promised all that the Father hath if he magnifies his priesthood.

*These blessings are to be shared with and by every righteous sister in the Church. A man can have no greater incentive or hope or strength in the priesthood than to know that his mother, his sisters, his wife, and his children have the utmost confidence in his righteous exercise of the priesthood and his love of the Godhead. They then have complete faith that he will magnify his priesthood and thus bless them in many ways, including pointing the way towards exaltation.

You see, in order for the doctrine of the priesthood to distil upon our souls as the dew from heaven, we must *become comfortable* in using this Divine power righteously. This means that we will truly *act for God* when asked to do so. It means that we will seldom ever *pray over* an individual but *pray for* that person.

A priesthood holder who prays over others simply, and incorrectly, puts the burden for the blessings back on to the Father. One who prays for others serves as the voice of the Savior Himself. He has taken time, when possible, to find out the will of the Father in behalf of that person. Then, he has the courage and confidence to act in place of the Son, which is exactly why the priesthood was entrusted to him in the first place.

Such a righteous holder and user of the priesthood invokes upon the individual all of the appropriate blessings. He can do this, without fear, because he knows that he represents the Father and the Son, **and that he is doing exactly what these two members of the Godhead would do if they were personally present.**

In regard to this critically important difference between praying over or for a person, we need to ponder the words of Nephi, *"Do ye not remember the things which the Lord hath*

Chapter 1   197

said? — If ye will not harden your hearts, and ask me in faith, believing that ye shall receive, with diligence in keeping my commandments, surely these things shall be made known unto you" (see 1 Nephi 15:11). If we follow Nephi's rationale, we will truly become disciples of Christ acting with confidence in His place under His direction.

Ask in faith! How many times has that or similar instructions been given? There are at least thirty of such occasions in the Doctrine and Covenants alone. Need we be afraid to ask! Certainly not, if we are full of charity, faith, and virtue.

This means that we are to be as personally righteous as implied by the Lord concerning Nephi: *"And now, because thou has done this with such unwearyingness, behold, I will bless thee forever; and I will make thee mighty in word and in deed, in faith and in works; yea, even that all things shall be done unto thee according to thy word, **for thou shalt not ask that which is contrary to my will"** (see Helaman 10:5).

It is a beautiful feeling to know that you can act for and in behalf of God, and not do or say anything contrary to His will. It is not only an exquisite feeling, it is also a very comfortable one. When it is repeated over and over again, your confidence waxes stronger and stronger in making the right choices as you perform priesthood functions and blessings. However, do not ever forget from whence comes your authority and power.

You will make the right choices if you are living a personally righteous life by focusing on spiritual things. The story of Martha and Mary is illustrative of this. Martha was encumbered about much serving of Jesus and His disciples. Mary sat at His feet to hear His word. Martha asked the Lord why He apparently did not care that Mary had left her alone in her serving tasks. The Savior replied: *" . . .Martha, Martha, thou art careful and troubled about many things: but one thing is needful: and Mary has chosen that good part, which shall not be taken away from her"* (see Luke 10:38—42).

Like Martha, we often find ourselves occupied by what is routine and temporal. Thus, we make Martha—like decisions, develop Martha—like values, and do Martha—like actions, because we have developed Martha—like emotions. When this happens, we fail to cherish the opportunities which are unique and spiritual — the Mary—like decisions, emotions, and actions.

When we use the priesthood of God in Martha—like ways, we do not bless people, and we tend to perform as if we were robots by mouthing words without much spirit. We pray over people. To use the priesthood of God correctly, we have to use it in Mary—like ways. When we do, we pray for people under the influence of the Holy Ghost; we know God's will concerning them; and we are not going to do or ask for anything contrary to His desires.

This gives us supreme confidence to act for and in behalf of God over and over again. We become partners with the Father. How truly comfortable that feels! How binding in heaven it is as we fulfill the contract that we have with our own Heavenly Father!

We will be comfortable in His presence and we will be able to rejoice in the doctrine of the priesthood as it distils upon our souls if we fulfill these five responsibilities:

1. Faithfully do all of the things that we know we should do and avoid all of those things which are repugnant to the Spirit of the Lord.

2. Study the teachings of the prophets in the scriptures and elsewhere. Apply that which we learn to the improvement of our lives.

3. Conduct our own lives in such a manner that we are continually in harmony with the Holy Ghost. Such harmony will be so snug that we may even wonder, on occasion, if the Holy Ghost is with us. In many instances, it is only when the Spirit has left us that we can realize how closely we were associated with the Lord.

Chapter 1 199

4. Participate fully in sustaining and carrying out the work of the Kingdom of God. This includes being obedient to the rules, commandments, and covenants of the Gospel. It encompasses the Laws of Sacrifice and Consecration. These two laws are celestial covenants — and nothing less.

5. Sustain the leaders of the Church who are duly appointed by proper authority. This is a profound part of honoring our priesthood. If you negatively question your leaders, you raise many serious doubts concerning your own authority in the minds of those who look to you for their authority to act.

Elder Bruce R. McConkie has very beautifully outlined for us ten blessings of the priesthood. He stated that each of these blessings are available to every righteous servant of the Lord.

*We are members of the only true and living Church upon the face of the whole earth, and we have received the fulness of the everlasting gospel (see D&C 84:19).

*We have received the gift of the Holy Ghost, and we are entitled to receive the gifts of the Spirit — those wondrous spiritual endowments which set us apart from the world and raise us above carnal things (see D&C 107:18—19).

*We can be justified by the Spirit, have dross and evil burned out of us as though by fire, become clean and spotless, and be fit to dwell with the gods and angels (see Alma 13:11—12).

*We can stand in the place and stead of Jesus Christ in administering salvation to the children of men (see D&C 45:32; 87:8).

*We have power to become the sons of God [sanctification], to be adopted into the family of the Lord Jesus Christ, to have Him as our father, to become one with Him as He is one with His Father (see Moses 6:67—68; Romans 8:17,29).

*We can enter into the patriarchal order, the order of

200   Where Art Thou

eternal marriage, the order which enables the family unit to continue everlastingly in celestial glory (see D&C 131:1—4).

*We have the power to govern all things, both temporal and spiritual, the kingdoms of the world, and the elements and storms and powers of the earth (see JST Genesis 14:30—31).

*We have the power, through the priesthood, to gain eternal life, the greatest of all the gifts of God (see D&C 84:44; JST Hebrews 7:13; D&C 76:54—59).

*We have power to make our calling and election sure, so that while we yet dwell in mortality, having overcome the world and been true and faithful in all things, we shall be sealed up unto eternal life in the presence of Him whose we are (see D&C 131:5; D&C 132:49).

*We have the power — and it is our privilege — so to live that, becoming pure in heart, we shall see the face of God while we yet dwell as mortals in a world of sin and sorrow (see D&C 93:1; D&C 67:10—13).

Elder McConkie truly lived and believed in these ten blessings. In his last address to the people of the Church assembled in General Conference, he offered this stirring but humble testimony: *"I am one of his witnesses, and in a coming day I shall feel the nail marks in his hands and in his feet and shall wet his feet with my tears. But I shall not know any better then than I know now that he is God's Almighty Son, that he is our Savior and Redeemer, and that salvation comes in and through his atoning blood and in no other way."*

Such a powerful testimony surely fulfills the spirit of the scripture given at the beginning of this chapter — D&C 121:45. By being completely obedient, by having a fullness of charity, faith, and virtue, then as surely as the night follows the day, our confidence will wax strong in the presence of God and the doctrine of the priesthood will distil upon our souls in receipt

Chapter 1

of the eternal blessings of an ever—loving Heavenly Father.

We will have achieved the ultimate goal to which we have aspired. We will not have fallen short of the mark. Our motives will be pure. Our actions will be righteous. The reward will be ours —victory in eternal life in the presence of our most gracious Heavenly Father.

Where Art Thou

Chapter Fifteen

THE HOLY GHOST SHALL BE THINE?

D&C 121:46 — *"The Holy Ghost shall be thy constant companion, and thy scepter an unchanging scepter of righteousness and truth; and thy dominion shall be an everlasting dominion, and without compulsory means it shall flow unto thee forever and ever."*

Frequently, the statement is made that the Holy Ghost is bestowed upon us through the laying on of hands to be a constant companion to us. Unfortunately, that promise is not always carried out. Like all covenants and promises, the Lord has no need to break them. We are the ones who do the breaking when we fail to abide by the specific conditions of each covenant or promise.

By this standard, the Holy Ghost can only be our constant companion when we are living or acting in accordance with the conditions by which the Spirit must abide, as opposed by those we would place upon Him. For example, we are required to be virtuous. If we place ourselves in unvirtuous situations, there is no way we can expect the Holy Ghost to be there with us. This truth would apply if we were reading a sexually explicit magazine or attending such a movie. Like Jesus, the Holy Ghost cannot, indeed will not, dwell in unclean tabernacles, which term includes speech, conduct, places, situations, and appearances.

204   Where Art Thou

This scripture (D&C 121:46) tells us that the Holy Ghost *shall* become our constant companion. It is referring to a condition or state of righteousness that has reached a much higher level and intensity than that attained in every day living. This means that we are somewhere between being *fully* justified — cleansed from all our sins — and having our calling and election made sure through the more sure word of prophecy.

In Chapter Fourteen, a list of Elder Bruce R. McConkie's ten blessings of the priesthood was included. Blessing number nine stated: "We have power to make our calling and election sure, so that while we yet dwell in mortality, having overcome the world [justified] and been true and faithful in all things [sanctified], we shall be sealed up unto eternal life and have the unconditional promise of eternal life in the presence of Him whose we are."

In previous chapters, we stated that it is entirely possible for us to attain sanctification in this life. To many of us, this level of daily living seems so distant that it does not have much practical meaning for us here and now. One of the reasons for this state of mind is that we are not willing to change or we may feel that we cannot make changes at that particular moment. Yet the depth of thought and meaning contained in this scripture (D&C 121:46) indicates that sincere changes not only can but must be made. It also serves to demonstrate the great change in the level of understanding and wisdom attained by Joseph Smith between the time he visited the Sacred Grove and the writing of the letter in the Liberty Jail.

President David O. McKay stated that: *"Human nature* ***can*** *be changed, here and now. You can change human nature. No man who has felt in him the Spirit of Christ, even for half a minute, can deny this truth. You do change human nature — **your own human nature** — if you surrender it to Christ. Human nature has been changed in the past. Human nature must be changed on an enormous scale in the future, unless the world is to be drowned in its own flood. And only Christ can change it."*

Chapter 1

There is absolutely no doubt that what this great Prophet of the Lord said is true. We can make tremendous changes in our own human natures if we will give ourselves completely to Christ and His work. The Prophet Joseph Smith said, *"It is the first principle of the Gospel to know for a certainty the character of God, and to know that we may converse with him face to face as one man converses with another."*

The question that each of us must answer for ourselves is whether or not the price that we must pay in order to make the necessary changes in our nature to this extent is worth it. More than one person has uttered words to the effect that "this is how I am," or "you have to accept me as I am." The sad truth in that no one has to accept themselves as "they are." It is each individual who has to do the accepting of him— or her—self, then do the evaluating, followed by the changing.

But not any change will do. Change for the sake of change is about as valuable as no change. Change in the direction of Jesus Christ is, on the other hand, an entirely different matter. When you make that an orderly, planned, progressive change, you are moving steadily and surely towards making your calling and election sure.

*"When you climb up a ladder, you must begin at the bottom, and ascend step by step, until you arrive at the top; and so it is with the principles of the Gospel — you must begin with the first, and go on until you learn all of the principles of exaltation. But it will be a great while after you have passed through the veil before you will have learned them. It is not **all** to be comprehended in this world; it will be a great work to learn our salvation and exaltation even beyond the grave"* (see *Teachings of the Prophet Joseph Smith*, page 238).

The bottom rung of the ladder used in the illustration by the Prophet is faith. Each rung then ascends in outlined fashion thereafter. *"After a person has faith in Christ, repents of his sins, and is baptized for the remission of his sins and receives*

206   Where Art Thou

the Holy Ghost, (by the laying on of hands), which is the
first *Comforter, then let him continue to humble himself*
before God, hungering and thirsting after righteousness,
and living by every word of God, and the Lord will soon
say unto him, Son, thou shalt be exalted. When the Lord
has thoroughly proved him, and finds that the man is
determined to serve Him at all hazards, then the man
will find his calling and election made sure, then it will
*be his privilege to receive the **other [second]** Com-*
forter, which the Lord hath promised the Saints" (see
Teachings of the Prophet Joseph Smith, page 150).

Interwoven through these rungs in our ladder are the three
basis principles of study, prayer, and service. It is because of
the devoted application of these three principles that the rungs
of the ladder are successfully climbed one by one. *"How do*
you obtain a knowledge of the glory of God, his perfections
and attributes? By devoting yourselves to his service, through
prayer and supplication, incessantly strengthening faith in
him, until like Enoch, the brother of Jared, and Moses, you
may obtain a manifestation of God himself personally" (see
Lectures on Faith, Number 3, page 26).

Too often, we tend to view the process as an end in and of
itself. This would be akin to thinking that the love we
experience in marriage is an end. Love is not an end. It is a
journey and a process that must be kept aflame and alive or
our marriage would die a painful death.

Similarly, death is not an end. It is also a process by which
we can continue our eternal journey into the Spirit World and
the grave. It leads us from one place or status or condition into
a higher one, and it has substantial purposes and results.

Please study the chart below. It outlines the processes,
purposes, and results of the journey that begins with our
baptism into the Church of Jesus Christ of Latter—Day Saints,
and that should end with Exaltation in the Celestial Kingdom.

Chapter 1

PROCESS DIAGRAM LEADING TO EXALTATION

PROCESS	PURPOSE	RESULT
BAPTISM	KEEP ALL COMMANDMENTS	GIFT OF THE HOLY GHOST
HOLY GHOST	REBIRTH-BECOME NEW CREATURE CLEANSING VIA REPENTANCE	BECOME JUSTIFIED
JUSTIFICATION	ENDURE CHASTENING OVERCOMING ALL PERSONAL SIN	BECOME COMPLETELY CLEAN
ATONEMENT	BY HIS BLOOD WE ARE SANCTIFIED	RECEIVE THE PRIESTHOOD GIFT OF RESURRECTION
PLAN OF SALVATION	WAY BY WHICH WE RETURN TO OUR FATHER	SANCTIFICATION
SANCTIFICATION (RIGHTS OF PRIESTHOOD) (PRINCIPLES OF RIGHT-EOUSNESS) (POWERS OF HEAVEN)	PURIFICATION BEFORE CHRIST (KEYS, AUTHORITY, COVENANTS) (CHRIST-LIKE ATTRIBUTES) (GIFTS FROM GOD)	CALLING AND ELECTION MADE SURE
CALLING AND ELECTION MADE SURE	SEE THE FACE OF GOD BE ACCEPTED AND TAUGHT BY JESUS HIMSELF	MORE SURE WORD OF PROPHECY
ETERNAL FAMILY	COVENANTS MADE PERMANENT	EXALTATION IN THE CELESTIAL KINGDOM

The first step in that eternal journey is baptism. In Matthew we read, *"I indeed baptize you with water unto repentance: but he that cometh after me is mightier that I, whose shoes I am not worthy to bear; he shall baptize you with the Holy Ghost, and with fire. "* (see Matthew 3:11). Baptism in water by immersion washes away sin and iniquity while baptism by the Holy Ghost by spiritual immersion burns the sin and iniquity out of our souls. In reality then, there are two baptisms for each one of us, and both of these are necessary to reject both the sins committed before baptism and those we commit after baptism, if we properly and fully repent.

208   Where Art Thou

"Baptism by water is but half a baptism, and is good for nothing without the other half — that is, the baptism by the Holy Ghost. The baptism of water, without the baptism of fire and the Holy Ghost attending it, is of no use; they are necessarily and inseparately connected. An individual must be born of the water and the Spirit in order to get into the Kingdom of God" (see *Teachings of the Prophet Joseph Smith*, pp. 314,360).

It should be thusly evident that the need we have for the Holy Ghost is a very sincere and meaningful one. Perhaps we take this precious gift too lightly. The Lord certainly showed that He did not when He taught, *"And no unclean thing can enter into his kingdom; therefore nothing entereth into his rest save it be those who have washed their garments in my blood, because of their faith, and the repentance of all their sins, and their faithfulness unto the end. Now this is the commandment: Repent, all ye ends of the earth and come unto me and be baptized in my name, that ye may be sanctified by the reception of the Holy Ghost, that ye may stand spotless before me at the last day"* (see 3 Nephi 27:19—20).

The process whereby we can be sanctified begins with our becoming spotless or free from sin; in other words, we are being justified. This is not possible until we receive the Gift of the Holy Ghost by the laying on of hands by one who has the proper authority. The Holy Ghost must confirm us to our Savior who, in turn, must introduce or affirm us to our Heavenly Father. These confirmations certify our worthiness and cleanliness. Before the Holy Ghost can begin such an introduction, we must have received all of the rights of the priesthood; that is, all ordinances essential to exaltation must be entered into and performed in righteousness.

Once we have committed ourselves to becoming justified, there are several fundamental points that we must keep in proper perspective. In viewing these, you are strongly encouraged to use funnel vision, as previously discussed.

Chapter 1   209

*Justification, in and by itself, does not assure us of celestial glory.

*We may still fall from grace and depart from the living God (see 2 Peter 2:20—22; D&C 20:32).

*Our quest for exaltation is a gradual, life—long process that takes us through justification, sanctification, and making our calling and election sure.

*Justification requires faith in Christ as well as continued good works and endurance to the end. *"Ye see then how that by works a man is justified, and not by faith only"* (see James 2:24).

*The Light of Christ is given to us to teach us the difference between right and wrong. This gives us a headstart towards justification (see 2 Nephi 2:5).

*The Holy Scriptures repeatedly associate justification with repentance, acts of charity, remaining guiltless, and service.

If you will examine the chart on page 207, you will see that the next process we must examine on our journey towards exaltation is that of the Atonement. This has to be the single—most important event in the history of mankind. It may also be the least understood and appreciated.

The reason that we lack in—depth knowledge about the Atonement is because we tend to feel rather strongly that we cannot become perfect in this life. If we cannot become perfect, why make much of an effort to understand the Lord's gift to us? Hence, our lack of knowledge. If we routinely accept the premise that lack or perfection is a fact of life, we provide ourselves with an excuse to be imperfect, both in knowledge and in works.

210 Where Art Thou

Then again, after all of our efforts, we must rely on the Lord to sanctify us, and we may not be too sure that He will. Regardless of our reasons for not studying the Atonement in great detail, if we do not make it meaningful for ourselves, who will?

Moroni truly understood this great event. He wrote, *"Yea, come unto Christ, and be perfected in him, and deny yourselves of all ungodliness; and if ye shall deny yourselves of all ungodliness, and love God with all your might, mind and strength, then is his grace sufficient for you, that by his grace ye may be perfect in Christ; and if by the grace of God ye are perfect in Christ, ye can in nowise deny the power of God"* (see Moroni 10:32).

After the fall of Adam and Eve, our Heavenly Father promised them a Savior in order to overcome death and to prepare the way for our return to God's presence. By itself, however, our righteousness could never make us perfect as our Father in Heaven is perfect. But through the Atonement of Christ and the influence of the Holy Ghost, we can become sanctified and made perfect.

It is in this part of the process that the Sacrament becomes much more meaningful. You are invited to carefully assess the opening part of both prayers: *"O God, the Eternal Father, we ask thee in the name of thy Son, Jesus Christ, to bless and **sanctify** this bread [water] to the souls of all those who . . ."* The implications here are that we should be striving to become clean and sanctified for we are partaking of sanctified bread and water each week. This is what the Lord meant when He warned us not to be partaking of the Sacrament unworthily; in other words, putting sanctified bread and water into a physical body that is at least not striving to become sanctified.

Step number five in our process diagram pertains to the Plan of Salvation which is the system and means provided whereby we might accomplish all of the steps or procedures necessary to become worthy of a celestial inheritance. *"And*

Chapter 1   211

inasmuch as they do repent and receive the fulness of my gospel, and become sanctified, I will stay mine hand in judgment" (see D&C 39:18). The fulness of the gospel is the plan of salvation as encompassed in the new and everlasting covenant.

Elder Marion G. Romney said: *"With complete surrender to the spirit of the Gospel, let us, honestly and without guile, search our own souls and find the weakness which presently impede our upward climb to eternal life."* If we follow this sound advice, we will make every effort to study the principles of the new and everlasting covenant, and then earnestly strive to live them in our daily lives.

The sixth step in our process diagram involves sanctification, including the rights of the priesthood, the principles of righteousness, and the powers of heaven. You are invited to restudy this process as it is given in Chapter Three. For a quick review, a few points are worthy of consideration.

*The rights of the priesthood are the keys and covenants pertaining to the exercise of the authority of God as delegated to man. They can only be fully realized and understood in the temples of the Lord.

*We learn God's plan line upon line, precept upon precept, here a little, there a little.

*The covenants include instructive techniques which the Lord uses to teach us the Plan of Salvation.

*"*The nearer man approaches perfection, the clearer are his views and the greater are his enjoyments, till he has overcome the evils of life and lost every desire for sin"* (see *Teachings of the Prophet Joseph Smith*, p. 51).

*Malachi referred to Jesus Christ as a *"refiner's fire"* who would purify the priesthood *"and purge them as gold and silver"* (see Malachi 3:2—3).

212   Where Art Thou

*The Lord stated that: *"The power and authority of the higher, or Melchizedek Priesthood, is to hold the keys of all the spiritual blessings of the church — to have the privilege of receiving the mysteries of the kingdom of heaven, to have the heavens opened unto them, to commune with the general assembly and church of the Firstborn, and to enjoy the communion and presence of God the Father, and Jesus the mediator of the new covenant"* (see D&C 107:18—19).

*The Church of the Firstborn are members who have a right to commune with those who dwell in the Celestial Kingdom because their calling and election has been made sure (see D&C 93:21—22).

"The principles of righteousness are those Godlike virtues which connect us with the powers of heaven. [These] principles are [those] values which we all know we should seek after. Our objective is to attain a 'Divine nature' as taught by Peter in 2 Peter Chapters 1 to 3 inclusive" (President Ezra Taft Benson).

*The powers of heaven are those gifts given by God to righteous members. They include the blessings, powers, and promises attendant to the Priesthood.

*Without these powers, the power of Godliness is not manifested unto men in the flesh and no man can see the face of God, even the Father, and live (see D&C 84:20—21).

*The powers of heaven are those which hold the keys of the mysteries of the Kingdom of God and which make our temple covenants permanent in eternity.

Step seven on our process diagram is to make our calling and election sure. Since this is the main study of this chapter, we need to now consider a number of important facts, principles, and situations.

When a person has received the preparatory Gospel and

Chapter 1

has been justified, as well as sanctified to a sufficiently high degree, it is then possible for that individual to make his or her calling and election sure, so that he or she receives an actual guarantee of those blessings in the resurrection. The sealing power then becomes functional in that person's behalf, and in this upper echelon of the Gospel plan, the individual receives what we call "the more sure word of prophecy." In the words of the Prophet Joseph Smith, this *"is for him to know by the Spirit of revelation and prophecy that his calling and election has been made sure."*

The end purpose of the Gospel is to provide a means for those who are truly faithful to endure to the end, and we must endure to the end if we want to make our calling and election sure. Joseph Smith repeatedly exhorted the members to continue to call upon God in prayer and to be more faithful in rendering service in order to receive the more sure word of prophecy. He also strongly advised that we be patient as we wait for the blessing to be bestowed upon us by the Lord.

Why should such a blessing be so desirable? The answer, of course, is that we must continue through this entire process on our journey to Exaltation, which is our ultimate goal. But wait! That answer, while true and beautiful, does not open to our view the magnificent exquisiteness of the accompanying blessings as we make our calling and election sure.

In order to obtain a glimpse from one who experienced this exquisiteness, let us read the words of Joseph Smith. First, however, the Lord told that great Prophet: *"For I am the Lord thy God, and will be with thee even unto the end of the world, and through all eternity; for verily I seal upon you your exaltation and prepare a throne for you in the kingdom of my Father, with Abraham your father"* (see D&C 132:49). As a result of this bestowal, Joseph Smith had his calling and election made sure.

The Prophet, then, was well qualified through personal experience to teach us about this subject. He said, *"When a*

214   Where Art Thou

*person has his calling and election made sure, the Lord will teach him **face to face** and he will have a perfect knowledge of the mysteries of the Kingdom of God (see D&C 88:66—68). When any person obtains this last Comforter, he will have the **personage of Jesus Christ to attend him**, or appear to him from time to time, and even **He will manifest the Father unto him,** and they will take up their abode with him, and their visions will be opened unto him, and **the Lord will teach him face to face until he has a perfect knowledge of all things"** (see Teachings of the Prophet Joseph Smith, p. 151).*

There are two ways or procedures whereby we may reach this magnificently high level of personal achievement. They are:

1. We must endure the Gospel program until the end of our mortal probations and, if we have aimed at the highest possible or ultimate goal, we will have eternal life as defined in the above cited quotation by Joseph Smith. We have to always be sure that we are in the right place doing the right thing for the right reasons. Otherwise, we become like the man who struggled to place his tall ladder against the wall and worked long hours at his appointed tasks, only to find out much later that his ladder was leaning against the wrong wall.

We are told in Nephi that, *"And now, my beloved brethren, after ye have gotten into this strait and narrow path, I would ask if all is done? Behold, I say unto you, Nay; for ye have not come thus far save it were by the word of Christ with unshaken faith in him, relying wholly upon the merits of him who is mighty to save. Wherefore, ye must press forward with a steadfastness in Christ, having a perfect brightness of hope, with a love of God and of all men. Wherefore, if ye press forward, feasting upon the word of Christ, and endure to the end, behold, thus saith the Father: Ye shall have eternal life"* (see 2 Nephi 31:19—20).

Chapter 1   215

We endure by:

*fasting and praying purposefully as often as is prudently wise to the end of our mortal lives.

*having faith in the name and mission of Jesus Christ and centering our lives in Him.

*following the example of righteousness set by the Savior and acquiring His attributes.

*keeping all the commandments and covenants. *"If ye love me, keep my commandments"* (see John 14:15).

*obtaining the mercy of Christ through being justified from our sins.

*suffering patiently the afflictions and problems of the world even to the laying down of our lives, if necessary, in order to be sanctified in Christ.

2.   If you are worthy to have your calling and election made sure now, then essentially the Lord will take your personal Day of Judgment from where it is presently scheduled and move it up to where you are now. This would be a sure sign to you that your salvation and exaltation are permanent decrees in God's Kingdom. Peter truly understood this great concept. This is what he meant when he stated that, *"For so an entrance shall be ministered unto you abundantly into the everlasting kingdom of our Lord and Saviour Jesus Christ"* (see 2 Peter 1:11).

When a person is worthy and has had his calling and election made sure, he is in a different state insofar as his or her responsibility is concerned. In relationship to the Lord, the person has received the highest blessings of the Gospel. Therefore, his or her responsibility to God is considerably greater and much more intensified than one who has not

216 Where Art Thou

received this great blessing. When you receive your calling and election made sure, you are sealed up to come forth in the morning of the First Resurrection and to receive the designated blessing of Exaltation in the Celestial Kingdom.

As a part of that blessing, you are sealed up against all manner of sin, except the sin against the Holy Ghost (for which you cannot be sealed), and the shedding of innocent blood. To a great degree, you really would have arrived at such a spiritual development in your life that you have come to hate sin and have enmity towards transgressions of all types.

Joseph Smith stated that a person cannot commit the unpardonable sin after the dissolution of the body and the spirit. It must be committed in this life, However, it is possible for you to sin after having had your calling and election made sure. If you do, then you must pay the price of those sins yourself. The Law of Justice will be applied personally to you. You will not be able to invoke the Law of Mercy. In effect, your sin will have suspended that law for yourself.

The Savior taught, *"And the soul that sins against this covenant, and hardeneth his heart against it, shall be dealt with according to the laws of my Church, and shall be delivered over to the buffetings of Satan until the day of redemption"* (see D&C 82:21; D&C 78:11—12; D&C 82:12—13,20; D&C 104:1—9). The covenant, that the Savior was referring to in the above cited scripture, is the one which is made between you and the Lord when your calling and election has been made sure.

There is one verse in the scriptures that is greatly misunderstood by many members. It is found in D&C 132:26. President David O. McKay said that this scripture was concerned only with those individuals who make their calling and election sure. He used the example that, if a person committed adultery after being sealed up unto exaltation, and if the law of the Lord were in full force and the Kingdom of God were

Chapter 1   217

operating fully upon the earth, that person would pay the debt for the adultery in its entirety by suffering the total buffetings of Satan until the debt is fully paid by the person who committed the transgression.

The blessing of having the calling and election made sure was bestowed upon a number of faithful members of the Church. For example, Newell Knight received this blessing at the first conference of the Church in June, 1830. From the records of the Church, we read, *"A vision of the future burst upon him. He saw heaven open and beheld the Lord Jesus Christ seated at the right hand of God, and had it made plain to his understanding that the time would come when he would be admitted into His presence to enjoy His society forever and ever"* (see *History of the Church, 1:85).*

Another example is found in the *History of the Church*, dated February, 1831. We quote: *"After prayer and singing, Joseph [Smith] began talking. He began very solemnly and very earnestly. Suddenly his countenance changed, and he stood mute. He seemed almost transfigured. He looked ahead — his face outshone the candle which was on the shelf just behind him. He looked as though a searchlight was inside his face. After a short time, he looked at us very solemnly as if to pierce each heart and then he said, 'Brothers and Sisters, do you know who has been in your midst tonight?' One of the Smith family said, 'An angel of the Lord!' Joseph did not answer. Martin Harris was seated at the Prophet's feet on a box; he slid to his knees, clasped his arms around the Prophet's knees and said, 'I know — it was our Lord and Savior Jesus Christ.' Joseph put his hand on Martin Harris' head and answered, 'Martin, God revealed that to you. Brothers and Sisters, the Savior has been in your midst this night. I want you to remember it. He cast a veil over your eyes, for you could not endure to look upon him. You must be fed with milk not meat. I want you to remember this if it were the last thing that escaped my lips. **He has given you all to me and commanded me to seal you up unto eternal life, that where he is you may***

218   Where Art Thou

be also, *and if you are tempted by Satan, say, Get thee behind me Satan: my salvation is secure."*

During the summer of 1831, in Missouri, the Prophet Joseph Smith sealed up the whole Coleville Branch to eternal life. In D&C 88:1—2, another group of men were sealed likewise. Orson Pratt, in August, 1833, in Charleston, Vermont, also experienced this same marvelous blessing.

In the journal of Heber C. Kimball, an entry in the year of 1839 reads: "I felt very sorrowful, lonely — the following words came to my mind — and the Spirit said unto me, 'Write' — which I did by taking a piece of paper and writing on my knee as following — *'Verily, I say unto you, my servant Heber, thou art my son in whom I am well pleased, for thou art called — be careful to hearken to my words and not transgress my law, nor rebel against my servant Joseph Smith, for thou has a respect to the words on mine anointed even from the least to the greatest of them all, therefore,* **thy name is sealed in heaven, no more to be blotted out forever and ever.'** "

Now please remember, as critically important as it is for each of us to have our calling and election made sure, it is even more essential that we be sealed as husband and wife. Since exaltation is not possible under any circumstances for single people, it follows that only a husband—wife team can attain this highest reward (see D&C 131:1—4).

In the case of Heber C. Kimball's wife, Vilate, the Church Patriarch, Hyrum Smith, laid his hands upon her head and gave her the following blessing — *"Beloved sister, I lay my hands upon your head in the name of Jesus Christ, and* **seal you unto eternal life — sealed here on earth and sealed in heaven,** *and your name is written in the Lamb's Book of Life, never to be blotted out."* With this blessing Heber and Vilate Kimball became eternal companions in Exaltation in the Celestial Kingdom, never to be separated ever again. Vilate Kimball earned this truly great blessing through her unwavering

Chapter 1   219

and totally loyal support of both her husband and the Prophet.

Many of today's youth have been promised in their patriarchal blessings that they will be responsible for preparing the Lord's Kingdom for His Second Coming. These young people not only have the right, but the responsibility as well, to prepare themselves to make their calling and election sure, and thereby to receive the personal ministry of the Savior, who is the Second Comforter spoken of in the Holy Scriptures. Each and every one of these young people are now being prepared to be administrators for the Christ when He comes to rule and reign again in the House of Israel forever. It is not a question of if they can do it. Rather, it is one of whether or not they will pay the price necessary to accomplish the task.

Can you make your calling and election sure? Obviously, it is completely up to you, for the Lord is no respecter of persons. *"Verily, thus saith the Lord: It shall come to pass that **every soul** who forsaketh his sins and cometh unto me, and calleth on my name, and obeyeth my voice, and keepeth my commandments, **shall see my face and know that I am"*** (see D&C 93:1).

Incentive can always be received from experiencing vicariously the spiritual endowments of others. For example, in Kirtland, Ohio, this moving and profound occurrence took place. Try to savor it as you read it. *"The heavens were opened upon us, and we beheld the Celestial Kingdom — many of the brethren who received the ordinances with me, perceived this same experience — we saw glorified visions, also angels ministered unto us as the powers of the High rested upon us. The house was filled with the glory of God, and we shouted 'Hosannah to God and the Lamb.' Some of the men saw the face of the Savior, and others were ministered to by holy angels and the spirit of revelation and prophecy was poured out with mighty power upon them"* (Joseph Smith).

The more sure word of prophecy means to be sealed in the Heavens and to have the promise of eternal life in the King-

220   Where Art Thou

dom of God, **and to know this by direct revelation**. It is done
by and through the power of the priesthood. You will be sealed
up against all manner of sin and blasphemy, except the
blasphemies against the Holy Ghost and the shedding of innocent
blood. Your exaltation is assured because you will receive a
fulfillment of the promises given in the endowment regarding
your becoming a King or Queen and a Priest or Priestess.

Everyone acknowledges that complete perfection is
not possible to attain in this life. Yet this is often used
as an excuse for giving up or not even trying. Common
sense would tell them that we cannot be perfected with
an earthly body. This also implies that total sanctification
is not possible in this life either. But neither of these
will prevent us from having our calling and election
made sure in this life if we work hard to become as
perfected as we can possibly become.

What joyous thrills accompany this blessing! Not the
least of these include the right to commune with those who
reside beyond the veil as well as with the spirits of just men
made perfect. With such thrills, we should lose all desire to
sin. In large measure, this will truly be the reality of the
situation. The reason for this is that we have successfully
fought the fight in becoming justified. Having won the battles
of overcoming our weaknesses and sins once, it makes little
sense to fight the same ones over and over again.

We all need incentive, however. Perhaps you may receive
some from this account: *"I would exhort you to obtain a
knowledge of the glory of God, His perfections and His
attributes by devoting yourself to His service, by prayer and
supplication, by becoming Christ—like. This means you must
endure the tests and temptations* [justification] *of this world
and look beyond the mark* [funnel vision]. *Then you shall
obtain a manifestation of God and **converse with Him face—
to—face as one man converses with another*** [calling and
election made sure]" (Prophet Joseph Smith).

Chapter 1   221

At the beginning of this chapter, we cited D&C 121:46. In it, we are told that our scepter will be an unchanging scepter of righteousness and our dominion will be an everlasting one. Throughout this chapter, we have examined what processes we must endure if these promises are to be fulfilled. If we prove our full and complete obedience, the Father has promised through the Son that we shall increase in knowledge, wisdom, and power as we go from grace to grace. Then, when we reach the level established by the Father, which is to have our calling and election made sure, the fulness of the perfect day will burst upon us.

This means that, through the glory and love of Elohim, we shall be blessed to become creators of heavenly sons and daughters ourselves. All powers, dominions, and might will be given to such successful individuals, and they shall be the only ones upon whom these great blessings shall be bestowed. They shall flow upon us forever and ever without compulsion because they have been successfully earned and graciously bestowed.

All others, no matter how learned or wise they have become in this life, will be restricted to lesser rewards or kingdoms. In such cases, the fulness, which accompanies the making of our calling and election sure as husband and wife in exaltation, will be absent. In other words, those earning lesser rewards will be assigned to the two lower kingdoms in the Celestial Glory, or to either the Terrestrial or Telestial Kingdoms. Only in the highest kingdom of the Celestial Glory can there be eternal, exalted married couples who have had their callings and elections made sure.

No one else will be permitted to pass by the angels and the gods who are set to guard the way to this tremendously glorified reward. **Do not let yourself be one of this latter group.**

222   Where Art Thou

Chapter Sixteen

WHAT POWER SHALL STAY THE HEAVENS?

> **D&C 121:33** — *"How long can the rolling waters remain impure? What power shall stay the heavens? As well might man stretch forth his puny arm to stop the Missouri river in its decreed course, or to turn it up stream, as to hinder the Almighty from pouring down knowledge from heaven upon the heads of the Latter—day Saints."*

As you read this scripture, does not the magnificence of it take hold of your heart and make you feel so glad, yet humble, that you are on the Lord's side? As well might a man stretch forth his puny arm to stop the Missouri River in its decreed course as to hinder the Almighty from pouring down knowledge from heaven upon us.

Have you ever seen the mighty Missouri River? If you have, the utter futility of even thinking about stopping it in its course with a puny arm would be that much more magnified in your mind. It is indeed a mighty river carrying much traffic and providing vast quantities of water for every conceivable purpose to thousands and hundreds of thousands of people.

However, the futility that may come to mind as you read this scripture was not what the Lord intended when He inspired Joseph Smith to write the communication from which

224   Where Art Thou

came Sections 121, 122, and 123 of the Doctrine and Covenants. (You should note that these sections have been accepted by the body of the Church, by vote, as revelation, and indeed they are such.) Yes, Joseph Smith was frustrated with the evil designs of his captors, but not with the work of the Almighty.

Likewise, we can become frustrated. In our case, most of our disappointments come either from our own perceived lack of ability and talent, or our inability to motivate or manipulate someone else to do what we want them to do. Such frustrations for us can be both righteous and unrighteous.

To avoid unrighteous, self—defeating behaviors, two actions are necessary on our parts. One is that we have to get the most we can out of ourselves. The second is that we must accept the fact that, while we can exercise great influence on others, we can never control anyone else but our own selves. Yes, we can expand very widely the **influence** we have on others in different situations, but we cannot **control** any other single person, unless we exercise unrighteous dominion or force.

In order to get the most out of yourself, the following few pointers are offered for your consideration.

*Focus on your potential rather than upon your limitations. Values placed on outside appearances, such as height, are self—defeating. Convincing yourself that you are not as witty or as smart or as clever as others is destructive. These types of actions always involve the sin of comparison. When you stand before the judgment bar of God, the Savior's questions to you will involve only you. President David O. McKay stated that they will include:

"What have you done with the talents given you in the pre—existence?"
"How did you fulfill your Church assignments?"
"Have you been honest and virtuous in all your dealings?"
"What have you done to contribute in a positive manner to

Chapter 1   225

your community?"

"Have you been actively engaged in establishing a Christ—like life with your spouse and with each member of your family?"

"Have you been true to your temple covenants?"

*Devote yourself to things you can do well. Too many of us judge ourselves on our I.Q., but that is the poorest measure of our talents and of our abilities to succeed. It is quite common to see unsuccessful individuals with a lot of talent. Many people get interested in using their talents, but when the going gets rough, they look at others who are supposedly more "successful," and they become discouraged and quit. Others are always looking for thrills, excitement, quick changes, or fleeting moments of glory. Yet there is always the necessity of trial and error as we repetitively learn more and more about ourselves. Every person can do some things well. No one was born without talents. The task is to discover and develop them.

The film "Cipher in the Snow" vividly pointed out the fact that an individual's I.Q. can be negatively affected if that person is placed in a "put—down" environment over an extended period of time. The reverse is also true. By discovering, developing, and using your talents in a positive environment, you increase your intelligence.

*See yourself as successful. Modern day psychologists suggest that we use a technique known as "imaging" or "visualization." In order to succeed, we must first visualize ourselves as a success, then work as hard as necessary to achieve it. The most successful athletes visualize every move that must be made before they make them. They go through each one in their minds so thoroughly that the actual performance is frequently another rehearsal. The plain truth is that when we burn positive images into our minds deeply enough, they become an integral part of our subconscious behavior, and we begin to succeed when we execute them successfully. This is how we become Christ—like. Soon there is no competition in our behavior with ourselves or others. This is because

226   Where Art Thou

we have instinctively imaged our Christ—like attributes and then we execute them with a very high degree of success, which, in turn, excites us to further repeating the entire process.

*Break away from other people's expectations. Liberate yourself from trying to be what other humans want you to be. God placed us here on earth to determine our own uniqueness through discovery and expression of our talents. He did not make us identical. He does expect us to become righteous, faithful sons and daughters, but not robots. However, the wisest people of all seeks advice and counsel from those who can be more objective than they can be about themselves. Such advice should be sought frequently, evaluated, assimilated or discarded, and improvements made at all times under all circumstances. Even when advice is rejected, good changes can take place within us because of the evaluative process we have endured.

*Build a network of supportive relationships. One of the surest ways to improve your self—confidence is to make sure that you have a lot of love in your life. We are not speaking of unhealthy, selfish, dependent love. Nor are we referring to the phantom love that comes from independent people who want to do their own thing by pursuing selfish desires, then pounding themselves on the chest, saying, "Look at me and how great I am. Love me for I am a success."

We are talking about strong, healthy, vibrant, and powerful interdependent relationships in which we draw love from others; we give love to others; and we all positively grow as a result. For example, our temple marriage must consist of a strong network of supportive relationships between husband, wife, God the Father, Jesus the Christ, and the Holy Ghost. How else can the husband and wife assist each other to be justified, sanctified, and exalted, including having their callings and elections made sure? In such a marriage, no ownership rights to each other have been transferred, but each gives and receives from the other partner so that each and both are edified into the highest realms of spiritual success in full

Chapter 1   227

cooperation with the members of the Godhead.

*Be proactive in your approach to life. The full responsibility for the success you want in life is yours and yours alone. It is very, very true that you cannot achieve that success alone, by yourself. But that does not remove the sole responsibility from off of your shoulders. You must make your life happen, and you must control the direction in which you are heading. Many, many helps are available from both mortal and immortal sources, including the ministering of angels (see Moroni Chapter 7). Few of these, however, will force themselves upon you. The major exception to this will, of course, be Lucifer who wants you to be as miserable as he is. The most devastating of all feelings is to feel lonely, unwanted, or unloved. You are wanted. You are loved unconditionally. You need never be lonely, if you are interdependent with the Godhead. But, the bottom line is: you must make it happen.

As our base scripture for this chapter states, the Almighty will pour down knowledge from heaven upon the heads of the Latter—day Saints. No wonder our beloved Prophet, Ezra Taft Benson, has encouraged us to read and ponder and study the scriptures, with particular emphasis on the Book of Mormon. Yet, he had to tell us that we were under condemnation because of our lack of learning the lessons in that great book before we acted with any form of dispatch.

Moroni experienced that attitude of *"A Bible, we have a Bible!" He wrote: "And again I speak unto you who deny the revelations of God, and say that they are done away, that there are no revelations, nor prophecies, nor gifts, nor healings, nor speaking with tongues, and the interpretation of tongues* [powers of heaven]; *behold I say unto you, he that denieth these things knoweth not the gospel of Christ; yea, he has not read the scriptures; if so, he does not understand them. For do we not read that God is the same yesterday, today, and forever, and in him there is no variableness neither shadow of changing?"* (see Mormon 9:7—9).

228   Where Art Thou

One of our Church leaders was seated on a plane next to a lady who, upon discovering who he was, proceeded to criticize the Church about prophecy, revelation, and Joseph Smith. She quoted Revelation 22:18—19 as evidence that there can be no new revelation after the Bible. Patiently, he heard her accusations and criticisms. Then he asked, "Do you pray?" The lady was defensive about answering but finally she did respond with a "yes." The Church leader then asked her what she prayed for. She replied that she prayed for guidance and comfort; whereupon, he asked her to explain that, if there is to be no new revelation after the Bible, why pray for guidance and comfort, since these are forms of revelation. After a deep silence, the lady admitted the folly of her arguments and accepted a copy of the Book of Mormon.

In reference to Moroni's concerns, we sometimes read the Savior's teachings and accept them as truth, but we do not specifically assimilate the details into our lives in meaningful, positive ways. An example of the need to do this is contained in Paul's writings to the Ephesians, *"Wherefore take unto you the whole armor of God, that ye may be able to withstand in the evil day, and having done all, to stand. Stand therefore, having your loins girt about with truth, and having on the breastplate of righteousness; and your feet shod with the preparation of the gospel of peace; above all, taking the shield of faith, wherewith ye shall be able to quench all the fiery darts of the wicked. And take the helmet of salvation, and the sword of the Spirit, which is the word of God: praying always with all prayer and supplication in the Spirit . . ."* (see Ephesians 6:13—18; also D&C 27:15—18).

The following explanation is offered. It was arrived at by applying funnel vision rather than tunnel vision to the whole plan of our Heavenly Father. You are certainly encouraged to ponder your own understanding of Paul's very important teaching and devise your own interpretations.

When developing your concept of the whole armor of

Chapter 1   229

God, you should remember that the basic reason for doing so is to be able to withstand the powers of darkness. When a person is so armored and then prepared with the proper weapons, that person is to be feared more than the enemies of light. Why? Because that individual is so powerful in faith and so strong in knowledge of the scriptures that Lucifer's barbs fall away without strength or damage.

There, in this diagram, rests the entire processes which God has established for us to follow. There is no other way, and it will never be easy, but it will be worth it. This is because, while the process of change is frequently painful, it is so expanding in personal growth.

We have to understand why internal changes are necessary; then we have to develop a strategy for coping with the resultant turmoils, emotional conflicts, and behavioral adjustments produced by those changes. A few suggestions that can be of help to you in coping with changes are given below the diagram. Develop your own strategy for coping with those changes that negatively impact you.

REFERENCE	SYMBOL	MEANING
Loins	Chastity, Virtue	Truth - Justification
Feet	Goals and Objectives	Preparation - Rights of the Priesthood
Sword	Word of God	Scriptures - Principles of Righteousness
Shield	Faith	Words - Powers of Heaven
Heart	Conduct	Righteousness - Sanctification
Head	Thoughts	Exaltation - Calling and Election Made Sure

*Be an optimist. The worst coper is the pessimist - one who is blinded by a negative attitude towards viable solutions. An optimist tends to see a setback as temporary; a pessimist sees it as a defeat. An optimist believes that things will improve if he does what is right; a pessimist feels that

230   Where Art Thou

everyone is against him, so why even try. An optimist is
generally happier, healthier, a better problem - solver, and one
who rebounds quickly. A pessimist is frequently beseiged
with emotionally - based physical complaints, a defeatest
attitude, and repetitive depressions.

*Take one step at a time. We have already referred to the
Lord's plan of learning of word upon word and line upon line.
Sometimes the dark clouds on the horizon prevent us form
seeing an optimistic solution, but by living one day at a time,
we can keep from being overwhelmed by the size and immensity
of the "big picture." We can cope much easier and more
successfully with small bites of the elephant. We tend to stop
worrying and start working. A good motto is to learn from the
past, live in the present, and plan for tomorrow.

*Keep the faith. This is the most vital ingredient in the
resiliency we need in order to cope with problems. Through
our faithful prayers, we can be taught that there is a pattern to
our lives (see D&C 52:14-15); and we can survive any test that
comes our way, if we will do our part. It is a well-known adage
that the Lord helps those who help themselves.
Perhaps the French poet, Guillaume Apollinaire, phrased
it best when he penned the following:

"Come to the edge.
No, we will fall.
Come to the edge.
No, we will fall.
They came to the edge.
He pushed them, and they flew."

*Take frequent inventory. To use inventories in our
lives is to develop hope because, as we analyze what has
happened to us, we can be much more realistic about our
perceptions on which we base our actions. Inventories also
give us courage to do what is right. Courage strengthens our
integrity and character. "*The disciple of Christ finds the truth*

Chapter 1   231

more sure and safe than a thousand compromises. Even though our lives be threatened, what of that?" . . ."No man [person] of principle can let his [or her] ideals or integrity be neutralized." . . ."Life without character and courage is little more than hollow existence. It brings shame, lust, and a thousand compromises."... "Courage is steel in the backbone. It is the perpetual friend and companion of the truth" (see Vaughn J. Featherstone, *The Disciple of Christ*, pp. 22-23).

*Commit yourself to action. It is not the commitment to a particular strategy that makes the difference in your life; it is the commitment that you possess to keep your vision sharply focused on your ultimate goal - Exaltation in the Celestial Kingdom. To do this, you must use funnel vision. Then, as you work backwards from that ultimate goal, each challenge and each covenant becomes that much easier to achieve. These become tempering, refining experiences rather than insurmountable Mount Everests.

Elder Paul H. Dunn has suggested three encouragements that we can use as we learn how to cope with, and to open up our minds to receive, this great outpouring of knowledge from the Father as promised in D&C 121:33. These same three encouragements can also be of significant assistance to us as we learn how to get the most out of ourselves when we fill our vision with the ultimate goal. This approach helps us greatly as we strive to cope with all of the changes that we must make, or endure within ourselves, as we work our way through the intermediate objectives in order to reach that ultimate goal.

*Reach Out a Little Higher! Perhaps you will recall the analogy of the large rubber band which is of very little use until we stretch it to its limits without breaking it. We must always strive to so stretch our abilities and talents by looking beyond our limitations and selfish desires, while, at the same time, not looking beyond the mark. If we constantly seek to stretch our status quo in faith, virtue, and charity, as well as other Christ-like attributes, our lives will become so meaningful and so

232   Where Art Thou

purposeful that failure would be the furtherest thing from our minds. We would not even consider the thought of failing to reach our ultimate goal.

*Try a Little Harder! Some years ago, an advertising slogan was used by the Church. It stated the simple concept of "Look Up!" As we applied that in our lives, we noticed so much more beauty in buildings, trees, clouds, birds, and skies. How little you see when your vision is towards the ground just in front of your feet! Challenge yourself to try a little harder by learning something new and beautiful from every experience, every speaker, every friend, every scripture, every temple visit. Reach out and up for learning and then act as if you are starved for knowledge. But, focus always on the search for truths about yourself and the holy Trinity. You can find them every where, but never in anti-Mormon literature.

*Reach Out a Little Further! This point is best illustrated by the story of the great Ted Williams who was the last major league baseball player to hit .400 for one full season. It happened in 1941. At the beginning of the last week of the season, his batting average was just above the magic .400. History was indeed in the making. The manager asked him if he wanted to sit on the bench to preserve his average, thus ensuring his great success. Ted replied: "If I'm going to be a .400 hitter, I'm going to earn the honor fair and square."

During that last week, Williams' bating average fell to .39955 which, when it was rounded off in the record books, would be entered as .400. On the last day of the season, with every one urging him not to play, Ted Williams still had the same attitude - he would work for the honor. When the last regular season game was over, Ted's batting average was .406. Truly Ted Williams reached out a little further and made history.

"Hast thou not known? Has thou not heard, that the everlasting God, the Lord, the Creator of the ends of the earth, fainteth not, neither is weary? There is no searching of his

Chapter 1 233

understanding. He giveth power to the faint; and to them that have no might he increaseth strength. Even the youths shall faint and be weary, and the young men shall utterly fall: but **they that wait up on the Lord shall renew their strength: and they shall mount up with wings as eagles: they shall run, and not be weary; they shall walk, and not faint"** (see Isaiah 40:28-31). He will help us reach further.

President Spencer W. Kimball stated, *"God does notice us, and he watches over us. But, it is usually through another person that he meets our needs."* What we have to look for is that we do not become so impatient that we begin to question our love for the Lord and His love for us.

Some years ago, a leading publishing company conducted a national survey. It revealed that the people of the world were in desperate need of a religion that would rebuild their faith in Christian living based on (1) the strength of their forefathers; (2) strong family relationships; and (3) centered on "Love thy neighbor as thyself." This same survey discovered that the basic concepts of The Church of Jesus Christ of Latter-Day Saints paralleled the religious needs that people were seeking. However, many such people are blinded by the craftiness of men and they develop many philosophies and arguments into which we may sink if we are not careful.

We are commanded to love God. He has a perfect love for us. He loves us so much that He has promised to forgive us of those things we do wrong and remember them no more, if we repent and come unto Him. The problem is that we cannot just love God in return, and let it go at that. We must translate that love into a proactive daily learning and living style that encompasses our neighbors, ourselves, our families, and the Godhead.

The basic need in the world today is for people to be taught that the true principles of love include a definite lack of personal selfishness. Jesus warned us that one of the principle characteristics of the last days would be that love among the

234   Where Art Thou

people would gradually die. He also taught that the lack of love would become so great in the last days that even some of the very elect in the new and everlasting covenant would be deceived and fall away - and all of this despite the fact that the national survey previously cited showed that people basically wanted what was right in the sight of God.

Jesus also knew that contention is of Lucifer and not of God. It is evidenced by a "me-centered" or a dependent attitude. Yet one of the most fundamental human needs in all of us is to be loved by others and to love others ourselves. These are emotions that are as basic to us as food and water, yet the pursuit of them often causes or leads us into contentions of one kind or other.

More often than not, we find ourselves judging the ones we ought to love unselfishly and, as a result, find ourselves loving them conditionally. We become selective in who, how much, when, and under what conditions we love; and this includes the love we bestow upon ourselves and the Godhead. We invoke restrictions where Jesus placed none. We "conditionalize" our love for others, yet we expect them to accept and to love us unconditionally as we prove ourselves. Such is the hypocrisy that Jesus hated the most.

The type of love Jesus demonstrated is exactly the same type we will develop if all of the principles of the new and everlasting covenant are applied in the pursuit of our ultimate goal - Exaltation. By examining the Savior's examples, we learn the following concepts.

*Day-by-day acts of service are very important in building cords of love that become so strong they can seldom be broken.

*A person who loves the truth loves honesty. It requires pure honesty to be true to all of one's covenants. Included in that love and honesty is the synonymous characteristic of trust. Some wait for others to earn trust before bestowing it.

Chapter 1   235

Jesus gave us all of His trust, and then said we could keep it through our actions.

*We jeopardize our future eternal existence when we love and sacrifice for that which is "me" or "I" centered. Jesus Christ acted in His own areas of responsibility and authority, but He never forgot nor failed to give credit to His Father for all of His blessings. His whole ministry was a prime, classic example of a "we" centered relationship - the exact same type we must develop.

*If we truly love Christ, we will love others as He loves us. We learn very quickly to hate (enmity) sin as we love the sinner. We choose whom and what we will serve, and we determine where our true emotions rest. Satan would have saved us but for the wrong reason. Truly loving the Savior guides and motivates us to be doing the right thing in the right place for the right reasons. What we love takes our time. That to which we give time becomes our way of life. Our daily actions and words demonstrate to others what that way of life is. If we aim too low in the pursuit of our goals, we may very well accomplish them but, when we arrive at any one of those goals, our ladders will be leaning against the wrong wall.

The beautiful messages contained in Section 121 of the Doctrine and Covenants can only be understood and achieved if our love for the Godhead, for ourselves, and for others is viewed with an eternal perspective using funnel vision. If we sacrifice and give our love for that which our Father in Heaven asks of us; if we continually examine and refine our perceptions by correcting our data bases and rejecting wrong understandings; if we are true to our temple covenants in all of our daily living activities; and if we love the Savior enough to acquire His attributes, our footsteps will be set securely upon the path that leads, through the process of making our calling and election sure, to our ultimate goal of Exaltation in the Celestial Kingdom.

"O God, where art thou?" Elder Howard W. Hunter

236   Where Art Thou

provides his answer to that question. *"He loves the Lord with all his heart who loves nothing in comparison of him, and nothing but in reference to him, who is ready to give up, do, or suffer anything in order to please and glorify him. He loves God with all his soul, or rather with all his life, who is ready to give up life for his sake and to be deprived of the comforts of the world to glorify him. He loves God with all his strength who exerts all the powers of his body and soul in the service of God. He loves god with all his mind who applies himself only to know God and his will, who sees God in all things and acknowledges him in all ways"* (see Conference Report, 1965 p. 58).

To which we say very fervently, **Amen!** How long can the rolling waters remain impure? The truth is restored. God lives! We find Him in pure places and revealed scriptures. **He is not, and never has been, lost!** He loves us unconditionally and He trusts us implicitly. He holds out His hands to us in meaningful ways that, if followed, offers us the reward of returning to live with Him forever and ever. These were the promises to us when Adam and Eve fell after partaking of the fruit. These remain His promises to us as long as there is one righteous person left on this earth to be taught the Gospel of eternal truths. we have earnestly tried to examine those truths in this publication. May His loving arms always embrace you as you embrace His truths.